Advanced English Dialogues, Stories, Vocabulary & More:
A Self-Study Course for Higher-Level ESL/EFL Learners

Jackie Bolen

www.eslspeaking.org

Table of Contents

About the Author: Jackie Bolen...6
The Tortoise and the Hare..7
Making Waves..9
Idioms #1...11
At School...13
Wasting Time..18
Exploring the Depths of the Human Mind...20
Idioms #2...29
Running a Marathon..32
The Bear and the Bee..34
Black and White..36
A New Hobby..38
Vanished Into Thin Air...42
The Development of Grammar...44
Greenhouse Gas Emissions...51
The Boy Who Cried Wolf..53
Core Values..55
Diving Into Coding..57
Idioms #3...61
When Pigs Fly..64
The Rise of Teotihuacán...66
Asking for Clarification..74
The Fox and the Crow..76
Get Into Trouble..78
At the Coffee Shop..80
Noise Pollution...84
Darwin's Theory of Evolution...86
Talking about a Customer...93
A Council of Mice..95
Knowledge-Based Economy..97
Swamped with Work..99
Feeling Under the Weather...103
The Nile River...105
Nice Weather and Weekend Plans...112
Idioms #4...114
The Frightened Lion...116
Online Dating..118
Taking a Trip...120
You can't Judge a Book by Its Cover..124
Hand Preference..126
A Dilemma..133
The Dog and His Reflection...135
Complaining about a Co-worker...137
The Daily Grind...139
The Last Straw...143
The Enigma of Dinosaur Extinction...145
Highly Effective...152
Idioms #5...154

A Bundle of Sticks..157
Hit the Books..159
At a Restaurant..161
Affordable Housing..165
An Introduction to Economics..167
Famine..175
The Frog and the Ox...177
Talking about a Company in Trouble..179
Flying for the First Time 181
Dumped..185
An Introduction to Music..187
Finishing Work for the Day..195
Idioms #6...197
The Ant and the Grasshopper...199
The Chicken or the Egg..201
Checking Into a Hotel...203
Break a Leg...207
An Introduction to Medicine...209
Lifestyle Changes...217
The Goose that Laid the Golden Eggs...219
Idioms #7...221
Negotiating with Another Company..223
Get Back At...225
Bite the Bullet...227
Art History 229
Bitter Divorce..237
The Crow and the Pitcher..239
Giving Someone the Cold Shoulder..241
Idioms #8...243
Bump Into 245
Good With Computers...247
Unraveling the Tapestry of a Nation...249
Save me a Seat..258
The Clever Woodcutter...260
Breaking Out in a Cold Sweat 262
Build In 264
In the Pipeline...266
Crafting Spaces, Shaping Worlds...268
No Pain No Gain...276
Idioms #9...278
The Gnat and the Bull...280
Swallow My Pride..282
Break Up..284
Evolution...286
The Wolf and the Crane..288
Wrap Up...290
Weather Forecast..292
The Fox and the Hedgehog 294
From Dawn Till Dusk...296
Fell Off..298

4

Emotional Wreck...300
The Frog who Desired to be a King...302
Eating Habits..304
Give Out...306
Business Trip...308
The Lion and the Mouse..310
Sitting on the Fence 312
Holding Up..314
Opening Night...316
Idioms #10..318
The Bell and the Cat...320
Go to War..322
Back Down..324
Chill Out...326
The Wind and the Sun..328
Goofing Around...330
Before You Go...332

About the Author: Jackie Bolen

I taught English in South Korea for 10 years to every level and type of student. I've taught every age from kindergarten kids to adults. Most of my time has centered around teaching at two universities: five years at a science and engineering school in Cheonan, and four years at a major university in Busan where I taught upper-level classes for students majoring in English. In my spare time, you can usually find me outside surfing, biking, hiking, or snowshoeing. I now live in Vancouver, Canada.

In case you were wondering what my academic qualifications are, I hold a Master of Arts in Psychology. During my time in Korea, I completed both the Cambridge CELTA and DELTA certification programs. With the combination of almost ten years teaching ESL/EFL learners of all ages and levels, and the more formal teaching qualifications I've obtained, I have a solid foundation on which to offer advice to English learners.

I truly hope that you find this book useful. I would love it if you sent me an email with any questions or feedback that you might have.

ESL Speaking (www.eslspeaking.org)

YouTube: (www.youtube.com/c/jackiebolen)

Email: jb.business.online@gmail.com

You might also be interested in this book: Intermediate English Dialogues: Speak American English Like a Native Speaker with these Phrases, Idioms, & Expressions. It has hundreds of helpful English idioms and expressions. You can find it wherever you like to buy books. Learn to speak more fluently in American English.

The Tortoise and the Hare

In the heart of a vast and enchanting forest, there resided a **tortoise** renowned for his unwavering determination and a **hare** known for his lightning speed coupled with a tendency towards idleness. One splendid day, the hare, feeling a surge of confidence, proposed a race to the tortoise.

The tortoise, ever steadfast, accepted the challenge, and soon the entire woodland community gathered to witness the spectacle. As the race commenced, the hare surged ahead with remarkable swiftness, leaving the tortoise trailing behind. Filled with hubris, the hare decided to take respite beneath the cool shade of a tree, convinced that victory was assured.

While the hare dozed off in leisure, the tortoise, persistent in his plodding pace, steadily closed the gap. Each deliberate step brought him nearer to the finish line, a testament to the tortoise's unyielding commitment.

The **lazy** hare awoke to find the tortoise in close pursuit and, in a sudden panic, **sprinted** toward the finish line. Despite the hare's accelerated sprint, it was too late. The tortoise, through gradual and determined progress, crossed the finish line before the hare, securing an unexpected triumph.

The assembled animals **cheered**, recognizing the profound lesson that diligence and perseverance can overcome the fleeting advantages of speed and overconfidence. Thus, in the tapestry of the forest, the tale of the tortoise and the hare wove a narrative of intricate moral complexity.

The Moral

The lesson of "The Tortoise and the Hare" is to keep going and not to be too confident. The story shows that even if you're not the fastest, if you work hard and don't give up, you can still win in the end. So, it's like saying, "Slow and steady wins the race."

Vocabulary

tortoise: A kind of turtle.

hare: A kind of rabbit.

cheered: Shouted encouragement and support.

lazy: Not a hard worker.

sprinted: Ran quickly.

Comprehension Questions

1. Why did the hare decide to take a nap during the race?
2. What was the tortoise's strategy during the race?
3. What happened when the hare woke up from his nap?
4. How did the other animals in the forest react to the outcome of the race?
5. What is the moral of the story?

Answers

1. The hare decided to take a nap because he was confident he could win easily.
2. The tortoise's strategy was to keep moving slowly and steadily.
3. The hare woke up to find the tortoise nearing the finish line, and he rushed to catch up, but it was too late.
4. The other animals cheered for the tortoise, amazed at how his steady effort had triumphed over the hare's overconfidence.
5. The moral of the story is that "slow and steady wins the race," emphasizing the importance of persistence and determination.

Making Waves

Jerry and Linda are talking about a situation at work.

Jerry: I don't want to **make waves** here, but I don't think Kim is making a good financial decision for our company.

Linda: Oh, I don't know. Maybe you just don't see **eye to eye**? I think she's done a lot of research and **knows what she's doing**. She's generally quite good at making decisions. It's why they pay her the **big bucks**.

Jerry: Well, I understand why you'd think that. You were **born with a silver spoon in your mouth**, just like Kim, and have never really been **short on cash**. Anyway, it's some **food for thought**!

Linda: To play the **Devil's advocate**, making big decisions is **second nature** to her. She's great at it!

Jerry: Hmmm...okay. Let's **agree to disagree**. We're never going to **settle** this I think.

Vocabulary

see eye to eye: Agree with someone.

born with a silver spoon in your mouth: Someone who comes from a wealthy family who doesn't have to work that hard in life.

food for thought: Something to think about.

make waves: To cause trouble.

devil's advocate: Someone who takes the other side in an argument.

knows what she's doing: Sure of something or do something correctly.

agree to disagree: To stop talking about something controversial when you can't agree.

settle: Decide or agree to something.

big bucks: To have a very high salary.

second nature: Something that someone does easily and well because they have done it so often.

Practice

1. My mom and I had to finally _____ because there was no way we could understand each other's point of view.

2. I'm not trying to _____ but I just don't agree with what's going on at my company.

3. I'm thinking about changing jobs. My boss and I don't _____.

4. My cousin was _____ and has never had to work a day in his life.

5. My younger brother's most annoying habit is his need to always play the _____.

6. That newspaper article had some _____ in it.

7. I've learned so much from my teacher. I can see she _____.

8. I was hoping to not have to _____ for that job because the salary isn't great but it's tough in this economy.

9. Skating is _____ to him. He's been doing it since he was three.

10. He has a ton of responsibility but that's why they pay him the _____.

Answers

1. agree to disagree
2. make waves
3. see eye to eye
4. born with a silver spoon in his mouth
5. Devil's advocate
6. food for thought
7. knows what she's doing
8. settle
9. second nature
10. big bucks

Idioms #1

About face

Meaning: A complete change of direction, either physically or in strategy.

Origin: From a long-standing military command and manoeuvre that's thought to have originated in the British Army.

"We'll need to do an *about face* here. There's no way we can keep going with our current plan."

"He was forced to do an *about face* after his company went bankrupt."

Above board

Meaning: A plan or business agreement that is honest and/or legitimate.

Origin: Thought to have originated from times in which pirates ran the seas. "Under board" was when pirates hid underneath the deck to trick victim ships. Above board is be the opposite of that.

"We need to do this whole thing strictly *above board*. Revenue Canada is watching our every move."

"Let's keep this whole deal *above board*. I want to improve your reputation after all those sketchy deals we did in the past."

Ace in the hole

Meaning: An advantage that is hidden until an opportune time to reveal it.

Origin: A poker term referring to a hidden ace.

"Tim is my *ace in the hole*. Nobody knows how good he is except for me."

"Seriously. You don't have to worry about this party. I have an *ace in the hole* that I'm keeping as a surprise."

A chip off the old block

Meaning: Describes someone who resembles one of their parents in behaviour or appearance.

Origin: Possibly dates back thousands of years and refers to a smaller piece of stone or wood resembling the bigger piece that it was taken from.

"Oh wow! Timmy is *a chip off the old block*, isn't he? He looks just like you your husband."

"My daughter is *a chip off the old block*. She wants to be a doctor as well."

Across the pond

Meaning: Refers to the Atlantic Ocean. North Americans refer to people from the UK as "across the pond" and vice versa.

Origin: Centuries ago, a pond could refer to any body of water. This was later adopted into an American/British idiom and used to refer to the Atlantic Ocean.

"What's going on *across the pond* these days?"

"Did you hear that we're opening a new office *across the pond*? I wonder who will be heading it up?"

Actions speak louder than words

Meaning: Action is more important than saying you will do it. It refers to following through on a promise.

Origin: Unclear, but it's thought to be three centuries old.

"I'm so tired of him doing nothing. *Actions speak louder than words* and he is all talk and no action!"

"Over the years I've learned that *actions speak louder than words*. You have to lead by example if you want your company to be successful."

At School

A teacher is talking to her students.

Teacher: Good morning, class! I hope everyone had a great weekend. Today, we're going to **dive into** a new chapter in our science textbook.

Student 1: Hi, Mrs. Johnson! I didn't understand the last lesson. Can you **go over** it again?

Teacher: Of course! I'll be happy to **break it down** for you. Let's **start off** by revisiting the key concepts.

Student 2: I'm a bit **swamped with** assignments from other classes. Can we **catch up on** those later?

Teacher: I understand you might be swamped with work, but it's important to **chip away at** your assignments to stay on track. We can certainly **pitch in** to make it more manageable.

Student 3: Mrs. Johnson, can you help me **sort through** these research materials for my project?

Teacher: Absolutely! How about after class? And for the rest of you, don't forget to **knock out** your homework by the end of the week.

Student 4: I heard we're having a group project. When should we **meet up** to discuss our ideas?

Teacher: Great initiative! Let's meet up after school on Wednesday to brainstorm and **nail down** the details.

Student 5: Thanks, Mrs. Johnson! I'll make sure to **look up** additional information to enhance our project.

Teacher: Excellent! If anyone else has questions or needs help, don't hesitate to **reach out to** me. Now, let's get started on today's lesson!

Vocabulary

dive into: To begin something eagerly or with enthusiasm, often referring to a task or topic.

go over: To review or examine something in detail, usually for clarification or better understanding.

break it down: To explain or analyze complex information into simpler, more manageable parts.

start off: To commence or initiate, often used at the beginning of a process or activity.

swamped with: Overwhelmed or burdened by a large amount of work or tasks.

catch up on: To bring oneself up to date or complete tasks that have been neglected.

chip away at: To make gradual progress by working persistently on a task, bit by bit.

pitch in: To contribute or help, especially in a collaborative effort.

sort through: To organize or arrange by categorizing or selecting, often used when dealing with information or materials.

knock out: To quickly and efficiently complete a task, often used when referring to homework or assignments.

meet up: To come together or arrange a meeting.

nail down: To finalize or clarify something, often used when settling details or making decisions.

look up: To search for information, references, or details, usually online.

reach out to: To make contact or communicate with someone for assistance or information.

Phrasal Verb Challenge

Fill in the blanks with the appropriate phrasal verbs:

1. I can't wait to _____ this exciting project and explore all its possibilities.

2. Before the exam, it's essential to _____ your notes to ensure you understand the key concepts.

3. The professor will _____ the complex theory in today's lecture, making it easier for everyone to grasp.

4. Let's _____ the day by discussing the main goals and objectives of the upcoming event.

5. The new intern felt _____ tasks on the first day, but soon adapted to the workload.

6. After taking a break, I need to _____ my emails and respond to the messages I missed.

7. Instead of feeling overwhelmed by the project, let's _____ it by focusing on smaller tasks.

8. We should all _____ and contribute our ideas to make this group project a success.

9. Take some time to _____ the documents and categorize them based on their importance.

10. If you want to _____ your assignments before the weekend, it's crucial to manage your time efficiently.

11. Let's _____ next week to discuss the research findings and plan the presentation.

12. Before we conclude the meeting, let's _____ the details of the budget for the upcoming project.

13. Feel free to _____ any unfamiliar terms or concepts you come across during your research.

Answers

1. dive into
2. go over
3. break it down
4. start off
5. swamped with
6. catch up on
7. chip away at
8. pitch in
9. sort through
10. knock out
11. meet up
12. nail down
13. look up

Comprehension Questions

1. What project does the speaker express eagerness to start?
2. Why does the student ask the teacher to go over the previous lesson?
3. How does the teacher suggest tackling the complex theory during the lecture?
4. What does the speaker propose doing at the beginning of the day in the dialogue?
5. How does the new intern initially feel about the tasks on the first day?
6. What is the importance of catching up on emails mentioned in the conversation?
7. How does the teacher advise handling the feeling of being overwhelmed by a project?
8. What collaborative effort does the speaker encourage for the group project?
9. How does the teacher recommend organizing and managing documents for the project?
10. According to the dialogue, what is crucial for knocking out assignments before the weekend?

Answers

1. The speaker expresses eagerness to dive into an exciting project and explore all its possibilities.
2. The student asks the teacher to go over the previous lesson because they didn't understand it.
3. The teacher suggests breaking down the complex theory during the lecture to make it easier for everyone to grasp.
4. The speaker proposes starting off the day by discussing the main goals and objectives of the upcoming event.
5. The new intern initially feels swamped with tasks on the first day but soon adapts to the workload.
6. The importance of catching up on emails is mentioned in the conversation for responding to missed messages.
7. The teacher advises handling the feeling of being overwhelmed by a project by chipping away at it and focusing on smaller tasks.
8. The speaker encourages pitching in and contributing ideas to make the group project a success.
9. The teacher recommends taking some time to sort through the documents and categorize them based on their importance.
10. According to the dialogue, managing time efficiently is crucial for knocking out assignments before the weekend.

Wasting Time

Kim and Sally are talking about summer vacation plans.

Kim: What are you up to **this summer vacation**?

Sally: Oh, every summer, we head to our cabin at Lake Minnewanka.

Kim: Wow! I didn't know you had a cabin there.

Sally: Yeah, we bought it **5 years ago** and **since then**, have spent **as much time as possible** there. It's the perfect place for **wasting time**, doing almost nothing.

Kim: Well, you need to make time to relax, right? That sounds **idyllic.**

Sally: Definitely.

Kim: When are you heading out?

Sally: Actually, the **day after tomorrow**. I'm **under the gun** for packing!

Kim: Okay, have an awesome trip! Don't forget about your old friends **slaving away** at work.

Vocabulary

this summer vacation: Usually refers to time off that people have from school or work during July or August (in North America).

5 years ago: Now is 2021. 5 years ago = 2016.

since then: After a certain point in the past.

as much time as possible: The maximum amount, taking into account restrictions like school or work.

wasting time: Not doing much.

idyllic: Tranquil; peaceful.

day after tomorrow: In 2 days. For example, today is Monday. Day after tomorrow = Wednesday.

under the gun: Feeling pressure, usually due to a time constraint.

slaving away: Working hard.

Practice

1. _____, I've been doing way better.

2. I'm going to Japan the _____.

3. I've been _____ on this project for months now.

4. I graduated from high school _____.

5. _____ is what summer vacation is all about!

6. Let's find somewhere _____ to go to for vacation.

7. Can you stay late tonight? We're kind of _____ here.

8. _____, I'd love to finally read those books that have been sitting on my nightstand for months!

9. I try to spend _____ outside. It's great for my mental health.

Answers

1. since then

2. day after tomorrow

3. slaving away

4. 5 years ago

5. wasting time

6. idyllic

7. under the gun

8. this summer vacation

9. as much time as possible

Exploring the Depths of the Human Mind

Understanding the complexities of human behavior and the intricate workings of the mind is the fundamental pursuit of psychology. As an academic discipline, psychology seeks to unravel the mysteries of thought, emotion, and behavior, providing valuable insights into the essence of what it means to be human. This introductory exploration into psychology serves as a gateway to a diverse and dynamic field that encompasses a **myriad** of perspectives, theories, and methodologies.

The Definition and Scope of Psychology

Psychology, derived from the Greek words "psyche" (meaning soul or mind) and "logos" (meaning study), is commonly defined as the scientific study of behavior and mental processes. This broad definition underscores the comprehensive nature of the discipline, which extends its reach from the observable actions of individuals to the **intricate** processes occurring within the mind.

The scope of psychology is vast, encompassing a wide array of subfields such as clinical psychology, cognitive psychology, developmental psychology, social psychology, and more. Each subfield focuses on specific aspects of human behavior and cognition, contributing to the richness and diversity of psychological knowledge.

Historical Foundations

To comprehend the evolution of psychology, it is essential to **delve** into its historical foundations. Psychology's roots can be traced back to ancient civilizations, where philosophers pondered questions related to the mind and behavior. However, it was in the late 19th century that psychology emerged as a formal discipline with the establishment of Wilhelm Wundt's experimental psychology laboratory in Leipzig, Germany, in 1879. Wundt's emphasis on the scientific study of **consciousness** laid the groundwork for the systematic exploration of psychological phenomena.

The subsequent decades witnessed the development of various schools of thought, each offering unique perspectives on the mind and behavior. From Sigmund Freud's psychoanalytic theory, which delved into the unconscious mind, to John B. Watson's behaviorism, which focused on observable behaviors, the early years of psychology were marked by a diversity of **theoretical** approaches.

Modern Perspectives

Contemporary psychology has evolved into a multifaceted discipline, embracing a range of perspectives that reflect the complexity of human nature. The psychodynamic perspective, influenced by Freud's work, continues to explore the unconscious mind and the impact of early experiences on behavior. The behavioral perspective emphasizes the role of observable behaviors and environmental influences in shaping individuals.

Cognitive psychology, on the other hand, investigates mental processes such as memory, perception, and problem-solving. Humanistic psychology emphasizes personal growth, self-actualization, and the pursuit of one's potential. The social-cultural perspective examines the influence of cultural and social factors on behavior, recognizing the interconnectedness of individuals within their societal contexts.

Research Methods in Psychology

The scientific nature of psychology is manifested through rigorous research methods employed to investigate hypotheses and validate theories. Researchers utilize various approaches, including experiments, surveys, case studies, and observational studies, each tailored to address specific research questions. The scientific method is a cornerstone of psychological inquiry, promoting systematic observation, data collection, analysis, and interpretation.

The Application of Psychological Knowledge

Psychology is not only an academic pursuit but also a discipline with real-world applications. Clinical psychologists apply their understanding of mental health to diagnose and treat psychological disorders, while counseling psychologists assist individuals in coping with life's challenges. Industrial-organizational psychologists contribute to workplace efficiency and employee well-being, and forensic psychologists apply their expertise to legal and criminal justice settings.

The Role of Nature and Nurture

A central debate within psychology revolves around the relative contributions of nature and nurture to human development. The nature-nurture debate explores the interplay between genetic factors (nature) and environmental influences (nurture) in shaping individual differences. Contemporary perspectives recognize the intricate interaction between genetics and environment, highlighting the dynamic and reciprocal nature of developmental processes.

Conclusion

In conclusion, this introduction merely scratches the surface of the vast and dynamic field of psychology. From its historical roots to the contemporary perspectives and diverse applications, psychology offers a captivating journey into the intricacies of the human mind. As we embark on this exploration, we invite you to delve deeper into the rich tapestry of psychological knowledge, where the quest to understand the complexities of human behavior unfolds with every discovery and inquiry. Through the lens of psychology, we gain valuable insights that not only inform our academic endeavors but also enhance our understanding of ourselves and the world around us.

Vocabulary

discipline: A field of study or branch of knowledge, in this context, referring to the systematic study of human behavior and mental processes.

perspectives: Different viewpoints or approaches used to understand and interpret psychological phenomena, such as the psychodynamic, behavioral, cognitive, humanistic, and social-cultural perspectives mentioned in the passage.

methodologies: The systematic procedures or techniques employed in research, including experiments, surveys, case studies, and observational studies, to gather and analyze data in psychology.

foundations: The fundamental principles or origins upon which a particular field, in this case, psychology, is built and developed, encompassing historical roots and foundational theories.

cognition: The mental processes involved in acquiring, processing, storing, and using information, a key focus of cognitive psychology mentioned in the passage.

psychoanalytic theory: A psychological perspective, pioneered by Sigmund Freud, that emphasizes the role of the unconscious mind, childhood experiences, and the interplay of conscious and unconscious forces in shaping behavior.

behaviorism: A school of thought in psychology, associated with John B. Watson, that focuses on the study of observable behaviors and the influence of environmental factors on behavior.

humanistic psychology: A psychological perspective that emphasizes individual potential, personal growth, and the pursuit of self-actualization as essential aspects of human experience.

nature-nurture debate: A longstanding discussion within psychology exploring the relative contributions of genetic factors (nature) and environmental influences (nurture) to human development and behavior.

scientific method: A systematic approach to research characterized by observation, hypothesis formulation, experimentation, data collection, analysis, and interpretation, used in psychology to study and understand various phenomena.

Vocabulary Challenge

1. Myriad, in the first paragraph is closest in meaning to:

    a) a variety

    b) a very large number

    c) a few

    d) a number of

2. Intricate, in the second paragraph is closest in meaning to:

    a) simple

    b) unknowable

    c) complicated

    d) mysterious

3. Delve, in the fourth paragraph is closest in meaning to:

    a) excavate

    b) learn a bit about something

    c) go

    d) thoroughly research

4. Consciousness, in the fourth paragraph is closest in meaning to:

    a) action

    b) reason

    c) awareness

    d) morality

5. Theoretical, in the fifth paragraph is closest in meaning to:

    a) based on ideas

    b) based on experience

    c) based on observation

    d) practical

Answers

1. b
2. c
3. d
4. c
5. a

Multiple Choice Questions

1. What is the definition of psychology?

   a) The study of ancient civilizations

   b) The exploration of conscious experiences

   c) The examination of environmental influences

   d) The scientific study of behavior and mental processes

2. Who established the first experimental psychology laboratory in Leipzig in 1879?

   a) John B. Watson

   b) Wilhelm Wundt

   c) Sigmund Freud

   d) B.F. Skinner

3. Which psychological perspective emphasizes the unconscious mind and the impact of early experiences on behavior?

   a) Cognitive psychology

   b) Humanistic psychology

   c) Psychoanalytic theory

   d) Behaviorism

4. What is a cornerstone of psychological inquiry that involves systematic observation, data collection, analysis, and interpretation?

a) Philosophical method

b) Experimental design

c) Scientific method

d) Observational approach

5. Which perspective in psychology focuses on observable behaviors and environmental influences?

a) Psychodynamic perspective

b) Behavioral perspective

c) Cognitive perspective

d) Humanistic perspective

6. Which term refers to the interplay between genetic factors and environmental influences in shaping individual differences?

a) Nature-versus-nurture argument

b) Genetic determinism

c) Environmental determinism

d) Nature-nurture debate

7. What is the central debate in psychology regarding human development and behavior?

a) Nature-nurture debate

b) Historical foundations

c) Scientific methodologies

d) Perspectives in psychology

8. Which subfield of psychology is concerned with workplace efficiency and employee well-being?

    a) Clinical psychology

    b) Counseling psychology

    c) Industrial-organizational psychology

    d) Forensic psychology

9. What term encompasses the fundamental principles or origins upon which psychology is built and developed?

    a) Philosophical roots

    b) Historical foundations

    c) Scientific perspectives

    d) Methodological principles

10. Which psychological perspective investigates mental processes such as memory, perception, and problem-solving?

    a) Social-cultural perspective

    b) Cognitive psychology

    c) Behaviorism

    d) Humanistic psychology

Answers

1. d
2. b
3. c
4. c
5. b
6. d
7. a
8. c
9. b
10. b

Idioms #2

Back to the drawing board

Meaning: A saying used when an idea or proposal is unsuccessful and must be revised or redone.

Origin: From the mid-20th century. It was first used in a cartoon where a plane came down and an engineer said, "back to the drawing board." The meaning is that the engineer needed to re-do the design of the airplane.

"Well, let's get *back to the drawing board.* We'll figure this out in no time I think."

"I have to go *back to the drawing board* with my deck plans. The city didn't give me a permit for the previous ones."

Bang for the buck

Meaning: Something that offers good value for the money you paid for it.

Origin: Bang = excitement and buck = money. Could be a play on Pepsi's advertising campaign from the 1950s, "More bounce to the ounce."

"We need to get more *bang for our buck.* Mason just isn't worth what we're paying him."

"That video game console isn't cheap but you get a lot of *bang for the buck* with all the games that come with it."

Barking up the wrong tree

Meaning: To accuse someone of causing a problem that they didn't cause.

Origin: From the early 1800s when dogs were used on hunts. Some intelligent animals would trick dogs into believing they were in a certain tree but they were actually in another one. This is why dogs would bark while standing under the wrong tree.

"Talk to Lindsey. You're *barking up the wrong tree* for this project. I'm not in charge."

"I'm so tired of Jed *barking up the wrong tree.* I haven't done anything wrong at all."

29

Be all ears

Meaning: To tell someone that they have your undivided attention.

Origin: Unclear.

"Go ahead. *I'm all ears.*"

"*I'm all ears.* Please let me know when you're ready to talk about this situation."

Be at a crossroads

Meaning: To be at a point where an important decision must be made.

Origin: Where two roads intersect. If you take one road, you can't take the other one.

"*I'm at a crossroads* in life since getting fired. I'm not sure if I should find another job or go back to school."

"My grandpa *is at a bit of a crossroads* after separating from his wife. I don't think he knows whether or not he's going to sell the house."

Beat the odds

Meaning: To win or succeed when it is not probable to do so or when the chances are low.

Origin: Most often used as a gambling term. It's often used with reference to horse racing or sports betting.

"He *beat the odds* and is now cancer-free."

"My brother wastes so much money! He always thinks he's special and can *beat the odds* somehow."

Bent out of shape

Meaning: To become angry, irritated, or upset.

Origin: Unclear.

"Tommy got *bent out of shape* over his son's teacher giving him a poor grade on his art project."

"My boss gets *bent out of shape* so easily—she got mad when I told her I needed an afternoon off for a dentist's appointment."

Be on solid ground

Meaning: Your decision or conclusion is solid, secure; a good decision that isn't considered to be risky.

Origin: From physical combat or war—to defend at a line to prevent invasion beyond the line.

"*She's not on solid ground* with that latest decision. I'm worried about what her boss is going to think."

"I think that *you're on solid ground* and honestly have nothing to worry about. Everyone knows that Tony is a terrible employee."

Birds of a feather flock together

Meaning: People tend to hang around with people who same similar interests or values.

Origin: First seen in the 1500s but the origin is unclear.

"It makes sense that most of your coworkers hang around together—they're all computer programmers. *Birds of a feather flock together.*"

"My son and husband love spending time together—they both like nerdy things. *Birds of a feather flock together.*"

Running a Marathon

Jerry is talking to his friend Linda about running a marathon.

Jerry*:* I'm thinking about running a marathon. I have **butterflies in my stomach** though. It's going to be difficult!

Linda*:* What? It'll be **a piece of cake** for you. You're **as fit as a fiddle**.

Jerry*:* I know I'm always **cool as a cucumber** when I start the race but then I get so tired in the middle. I eventually get a **second wind** though.

Linda*:* **Fingers crossed** that you'll **knock 'em dead**. I'll come to cheer for you!

Jerry*:* What about you? Did the doctor give you **a clean bill of health**? You can train with me.

Linda: I'm not quite **back on my feet** yet. Plus, I have **a lot on my plate** right now. I've been **working day and night** on this latest project. I need **a change of pace** for sure!

Vocabulary

a piece of cake: Something that's easy to do.

cool as a cucumber: Very calm or relaxed.

as fit as a fiddle: In really good shape.

second wind: Having some energy again after being tired. Usually applies to exercise or staying up late.

butterflies in my stomach: Nervous feeling about something.

fingers crossed: To wish someone good luck. Or, a symbol of good luck.

knock 'em dead: Do well or be successful at an event.

a clean bill of health: Healthy, not sick anymore.

back on my feet: Recovered, after a problem (health, financial, divorce, etc.)

a lot on my plate: Many responsibilities.

working day and night: Working all the time.

a change of pace: Something new or different.

Practice

1. Don't worry, I'm sure you'll _____.

2. Under pressure, Roger Federer is as _____.

3. I always get _____ before a test.

4. That speaking test was _____.

5. I've got my _____ waiting for the results of the SAT.

6. My grandpa is _____ even though he is 80.

7. My wife has been _____ to get the latest project done at work.

8. I hope I get my _____. I have lots more studying to do!

9. I'm hoping to get _____ after my recent job loss.

10. I'm moving to Costa Rica for _____.

11. I'm hoping that the doctors give me _____.

12. I'm going to have _____ this week at work.

Answers

1. knock 'em dead

2. cool as a cucumber

3. butterflies in my stomach

4. a piece of cake

5. fingers crossed

6. as fit as a fiddle

7. working day and night

8. second wind

9. back on my feet

10. a change of pace

11. a clean bill of health

12. a lot of my plate

The Bear and the Bee

In a vast and vibrant meadow, there resided a **formidable** bear and a **diligent** bee. The bear, with his thick fur and powerful stature, often roamed the meadow, while the bee, small yet tirelessly energetic, buzzed from flower to flower.

One sunny afternoon, as the bee was busy collecting nectar to create golden honey, the bear, enticed by the sweet aroma, approached with curiosity. "Greetings, dear bee," said the bear. "Your honey looks delectable. Might I have a taste?"

Understanding the bear's appetite, the clever bee proposed a friendly **contest**. "Certainly, Mr. Bear," replied the bee. "Let's see who can gather the most flowers. The winner shall enjoy the honey!"

Excited by the competition, the bear agreed, and they set off to collect flowers. The bee darted swiftly among the blossoms, while the bear, using his massive paws, **lumbered** around and carefully selected vibrant flowers.

As the sun dipped below the horizon, they tallied their collections. To the bear's surprise, the bee had gathered more flowers. The bee grinned and remarked, "You see, Mr. Bear, hard work and diligence triumph over size."

Impressed by the lesson, the bear nodded appreciatively. "You are right, industrious bee. I've learned that the effort we put in is often more important than our size and strength. Thank you for this valuable lesson."

From that day forward, the bear and the bee became steadfast friends. They shared not only the honey but also the beauty of the meadow, appreciating the different strengths each brought to their friendship. And so, in the vibrant meadow, the bear and the bee continued to live harmoniously, savoring the sweet rewards of cooperation and hard work.

The Moral

The moral of the story is that working hard is important. Even if someone is big and strong, someone smaller who works really hard can achieve success too. In the story, the bee showed the bear that effort matters more than size.

Vocabulary

contest: An event where people compete with each other.

lumbered: Moved slowly and awkwardly.

formidable: Large and powerful.

diligent: Showing care about what one is doing.

Comprehension Questions

1. Why did the bear approach the bee in the first place?
2. What challenge did the bee propose to the bear?
3. Who won the flower-gathering challenge, and how did they determine the winner?
4. What did the bear learn from the bee's challenge?
5. How did the bear and the bee's relationship change after the challenge?

Answers

1. The bear approached the bee because he wanted to taste the delicious honey the bee was making.
2. The bee challenged the bear to see who could gather the most flowers, and the winner would get to enjoy the honey.
3. The bee won the challenge by gathering more flowers. They counted the flowers to determine the winner.
4. The bear learned that hard work and effort are more important than size and strength.
5. The bear and the bee became friends, sharing not only the honey but also enjoying the beauty of the meadow together.

Black and White

Terry and Sandra are Biology classmates discussing the issue of cloning.

Terry: What did you think about the **lecture** today? Interesting, right?

Sandra: The lecture raised a lot of ethical questions for me about **cloning**. It's not a **black and white** issue. There are so many **shades of gray**.

Terry: Definitely. There should be way stricter standards for replicating living things. At the end of the day, it shouldn't only come down to the researcher's **values** and **ethics**.

Sandra: Yes, **it goes without saying**. But who will **develop** these standards? Universities? **Industry**? The government?

Terry: That **remains to be seen**. Likely it'll be a combination of those things. Cloning is still a very new thing.

Vocabulary

lecture: In a university or college, where a professor gives information by talking about it. Typically, a 2-3 hour class that is held once a week.

cloning: Making a copy of something.

black and white: There *is* a clear right and wrong.

shades of gray: There *is no* clear right and wrong.

values: Basic, fundamental beliefs about something.

ethics: Moral principles that govern a person's behavior or the conducting of an activity.

it goes without saying: It's obvious.

develop: Make something new.

industry: For-profit companies.

remains to be seen: The outcome of something is undecided at the current time.

Practice

1. That _____ was so boring. I think I fell asleep for a few minutes.

2. That company has so many issues I think because they have no core _____.

3. It's a difficult situation! There are no _____ answers here.

4. Do you think that in 100 years from now, _____ of humans will be possible?

5. The university is putting together a committee to _____ some guidelines about cloning.

6. I can't tell you what to do in this situation. It depends on your personal _____.

7. You can make more money in _____ jobs than with the government but the benefits aren't as good.

8. It _____ whether or not I'll pass that test. It was so difficult.

9. _____ that he's the best choice for an advisor but he already has so many students.

10. I enjoy studying bioethics but I don't like that are so many _____ for almost everything.

Answers

1. lecture

2. values

3. black and white

4. cloning

5. develop

6. ethics/values

7. industry

8. remains to be seen

9. it goes without saying

10. shades of gray

A New Hobby

Tom and Laura are talking about getting into shape.

Tom: Hey, Laura! What's up? I heard you're thinking about **taking up** a new hobby.

Laura: Yeah, I'm thinking of picking up painting. I've been **looking into** it for a while.

Tom: That's cool! I've actually been trying to **cut back on** TV and take up reading more. I found this interesting book I'm **digging into**.

Laura: Nice! I might join a painting class to **brush up on** my skills. Do you have any recommendations?

Tom: Well, you could check out the community center. They often run classes, and you might **come across** some talented artists to **pick up** tips from.

Laura: Great idea! I'll look into that. By the way, have you thought about **giving up** fast food? I've read it's a good way to get in shape.

Tom: Yeah, I've been considering it. I'm also planning to start **working out** regularly and give up on my sedentary lifestyle.

Laura: Awesome! We should team up and work out together. It's easier to stick to a routine when you have a workout buddy to cheer you on.

Tom: I'm totally on board with that. Let's **set it up** and not **back out.** It's about time we **shape up** and live healthier lives.

Vocabulary

take up: Begin or start a new activity or hobby.

look into: Investigate or research a topic or matter.

dig into: Thoroughly explore or immerse oneself in something, often a subject or a book.

cut back on: Reduce the amount or frequency of something, usually a habit or consumption.

pick up: Acquire a new skill or hobby, often informally or casually.

brush up on: Refresh or improve one's knowledge or skills in a particular area.

come across: Encounter or find something unexpectedly.

give up: Stop doing or quit a habit, activity, or lifestyle.

work out: Exercise.

set up: Arrange or establish something.

back out: Withdraw or fail to follow through on a commitment or plan.

shape up: Get better at something.

Phrasal Verb Challenge

Fill in the blanks with the appropriate phrasal verb:

1. After a long break, Sarah decided to _____ tennis as her new hobby.

2. Mark needs to _____ his computer programming skills before the upcoming project.

3. The detective decided to _____ the mysterious case to uncover the truth.

4. Due to health concerns, John decided to _____ his daily intake of sugary snacks.

5. Mary unexpectedly _____ an old photo album while cleaning out the attic.

6. Despite initial enthusiasm, Peter had to _____ his plans to organize the charity event.

7. The team decided to _____ a new system to improve efficiency.

8. Mike promised to help with the project, but he unexpectedly decided to _____ at the last minute.

Answers

1. take up
2. brush up on
3. dig into
4. cut back on
5. came across
6. back out
7. set up
8. brush up on
9. back out

Comprehension Questions

1. What hobby is Laura considering taking up?
2. Where does Tom suggest Laura look for painting classes?
3. What has Tom been trying to cut back on?
4. What does Laura plan to do before starting the art class?
5. What does Tom recommend for staying motivated in a workout routine?
6. What does Laura propose to Tom about working out together?
7. Where does Laura find the novel she is currently digging into?
8. What lifestyle change does Tom want to make in terms of physical activity?
9. What is the main reason for Laura and Tom wanting to set up a workout schedule together?
10. Why does Tom suggest giving up fast food?

Answers

1. Laura is considering taking up painting.

2. Tom suggests Laura check out the community center for painting classes.

3. Tom has been trying to cut back on fast food.

4. Laura plans to brush up on her painting skills.

5. Tom recommends teaming up with a workout buddy to stay motivated.

6. Laura proposes that they team up and work out together.

7. Laura finds the novel at the bookstore.

8. Tom wants to give up his sedentary lifestyle and start working out regularly.

9. They want to set up a workout schedule together to stay motivated and support each other.

10. Tom suggests giving up fast food as a way to improve overall health.

Vanished Into Thin Air

Amy and Chloe are talking about some criminal activity in their city.

Amy: Do you remember the story of that 2-year old boy who **vanished** into thin air?

Chloe: It was all over the news. I heard that he showed up at his mom's house in the middle of the night after 2 weeks, apparently **unscathed**.

Amy: It was the strangest thing. I heard that the police barely **investigated** it. They just assumed his dad took him. But there was no **evidence** of that at all.

Chloe: The investigation did seem rather **haphazard**.

Amy: They are pretty much **negligent**. Thankfully he's okay. I think we need to **reinforce** our policing system with some more officers.

Chloe: I'm not sure that's the answer. I think we need to **reform** the policing system and get rid of the **corrupt** people at the top.

Vocabulary

vanished: Disappeared quickly.

unscathed: Unharmed.

investigated: Looked into; examined.

evidence: Facts or information to prove or disprove something.

haphazard: Not carefully; lacking planning.

negligent: Lazy; neglectful.

reinforce: Make something stronger.

reform: Makes changes to improve a situation.

corrupt: A willingness to act dishonestly.

Practice

1. My keys seem to have _____. Will you help me look for them?

2. We need to _____ the management structure of our company.

3. I'm taking my doctor to court. I think he was _____.

4. You can go to war with your boss, but you won't escape _____.

5. Clean your room, but not in the _____ way you usually do it.

6. We need to _____ this fence, or it'll fall down.

7. I've _____ the matter, and I don't think Cindy did anything wrong.

8. Don't you think that all politicians are basically _____?

9. There's no _____ that she's been treating you unfairly. A feeling isn't enough.

Answers

1. vanished

2. reform

3. negligent

4. unscathed

5. haphazard

6. reinforce

7. investigated

8. corrupt

9. evidence

The Development of Grammar

Language, as the **bedrock** of human communication, has undergone a fascinating evolution, with grammar serving as a crucial element in its development.

Early Foundations of Grammar: Innate Understanding

At the **dawn** of language, humans exhibited an innate capacity for grammar. From the babbling stages of infancy to the formation of basic sentence structures, early linguistic development showcased an inherent grasp of grammatical principles.

Emergence of Written Language: Shaping Structure and Clarity

The introduction of written language marked a significant milestone, bringing forth rules and conventions to maintain **clarity**. Ancient civilizations like the Sumerians and Egyptians developed scripts, influencing the structuring of grammatical rules.

Latin Influence in the Middle Ages: Prescriptive Norms

During the Middle Ages, Latin became the language of scholars and **elites**. Prescriptive grammar manuals emphasized "correct" language usage, shaping grammatical **norms** in various European languages and establishing a foundation for linguistic standards.

Renaissance and Modern Grammar: Vernacular Languages Resurge

The Renaissance witnessed a shift from Latin to vernacular languages. This period saw a renewed interest in vernacular grammatical structures, with influential figures like William Lily contributing to the codification of English grammar. The printing press facilitated widespread access to grammatical knowledge.

Enlightenment and Descriptive Grammar: Language in Action

The Enlightenment era departed from prescriptive grammar, adopting a more descriptive approach. Scholars like Sir William Temple and John Locke observed language in action, giving rise to descriptive grammar that aimed to describe language based on how it was naturally spoken and written.

Scientific Inquiry in the 19th Century: Linguistics as a Discipline

The 19th century witnessed the formalization of linguistics as a discipline. Scholars like Ferdinand de Saussure and Wilhelm von Humboldt explored the deep structures of language, contributing valuable insights to our understanding of grammar.

Generative Grammar in the 20th Century: Cognitive Structures Unveiled

The mid-20th century brought about a linguistic revolution with Noam Chomsky's development of generative grammar. This theory proposed that innate cognitive structures in the human mind give rise to grammatical rules, fundamentally transforming our understanding of language.

Contemporary Approaches: Cognitive Linguistics and Beyond

In the present era, cognitive linguistics takes center stage, exploring the influence of cognition on grammatical structures. Researchers delve into how metaphor, conceptualization, and embodied cognition shape the very foundations of language.

Globalization of Grammar: English as a Lingua Franca

In the 21st century, grammar continues to evolve in a globalized world. English, as a prominent lingua franca, exerts influence on grammatical norms worldwide, reflecting the rich diversity of linguistic expressions in our interconnected world.

Conclusion: Grammar as a Living Entity

The journey of grammar is ongoing, adapting to technological advancements and reflecting the multifaceted expressions of human communication. Grammar remains a dynamic bridge connecting diverse cultures and linguistic traditions, contributing to the ever-evolving story of how we communicate and connect across borders.

Vocabulary

innate: Naturally present or inherent; something that is part of one's essential nature or abilities.

prescriptive: Relating to rules or guidelines dictating correct language usage; providing authoritative instructions on how something should be done.

vernacular: The everyday language spoken by ordinary people in a particular region or community, as opposed to a formal or literary language.

codification: The process of organizing laws, rules, or principles into a systematic and formal set of codes or regulations.

structuring: The act of arranging or organizing elements into a specific form or pattern.

revitalized: To bring something back to life, energy, or activity; to renew or reinvigorate.

formalization: The process of giving a formal or official structure to something, making it systematic or legally recognized.

departed: To deviate or move away from a previous practice or approach; to go in a different direction.

multifaceted: Having many different aspects, features, or perspectives; characterized by a variety of elements.

interconnected: Having connections or relationships between different parts; mutually related or dependent on each other.

Vocabulary Challenge

1. Bedrock, in the first paragraph is closest in meaning to:
   a) solid rock
   b) a foundation
   c) fundamental principle
   d) minerals

2. Dawn, in the second paragraph is closest in meaning to:

   a) the beginning

   b) the first appearance of light

   c) a time of the day

   d) the end

3. Clarity, in the third paragraph is closest in meaning to:

   a) confusion

   b) purity

   c) intelligible

   d) cleanliness

4. Elites, in the fourth paragraph is closest in meaning to:

   a) the rich

   b) the famous

   c) the educated

   d) the superior

5. Norms, in the fourth paragraph is closest in meaning to:

   a) a pattern

   b) something that is unusual

   c) how to act

   d) something unacceptable

Answers

   1. c

   2. a

   3. c

   4. d

   5. a

Multiple Choice Questions

1. What does the term "innate" mean in the context of language development?

    a) Learned through experience

    b) Naturally present or inherent

    c) Socially acquired

    d) Vernacular expression

2. In the Middle Ages, Latin became the standard language for:

    a) Everyday communication

    b) Vernacular literature

    c) Scholars and elites

    d) Descriptive grammar

3. What is the primary focus of prescriptive grammar manuals during the Middle Ages?

    a) Describing natural language usage

    b) Codifying vernacular languages

    c) Emphasizing "correct" language usage

    d) Analyzing linguistic structures

4. During the Renaissance, what contributed to the renewed interest in vernacular languages?

    a) Decline of written language

    b) Exploration of Latin

    c) Shift from Latin to vernacular languages

    d) Suppression of grammatical knowledge

5. What characterizes descriptive grammar as developed during the Enlightenment era?

   a) Prescribing language rules

   b) Focusing on innate cognitive structures

   c) Observing language in action

   d) Establishing a standard language

6. What is the key contribution of Ferdinand de Saussure to linguistics in the 19th century?

   a) Descriptive grammar principles

   b) Vernacular language analysis

   c) Exploration of deep language structures

   d) Codification of Latin grammar

7. What is the central idea behind Noam Chomsky's generative grammar?

   a) Language as a cultural construct

   b) Language evolves through experience

   c) Innate cognitive structures give rise to grammatical rules

   d) Language follows prescriptive norms

8. What does the term "cognitive linguistics" primarily emphasize in the study of grammar?

   a) Innate language structures

   b) Cultural influences on language

   c) Metaphors and conceptualization

   d) Formal grammatical rule

9. In the 21st century, English is considered a lingua franca. What does this mean?

   a) English is only spoken in France

   b) English serves as a global communication bridge

   c) English is a formal academic language

   d) English is limited to specific regions

10. What term describes the ongoing process of adapting grammar to technological advancements and reflecting diverse linguistic expressions?

a) Descriptive grammar

b) Innate language development

c) Codification

d) Grammar as a living entity

Answers

1. b
2. c
3. c
4. c
5. c
6. c
7. c
8. c
9. b
10. d

Greenhouse Gas Emissions

Sid and Drew are environmental science students who are discussing an issue.

Sid: Hey Drew. Did you hear that **greenhouse gas emissions** have gone way down since Covid started?

Drew: Oh yeah. I heard that. That's good news but I'm not sure it's enough to combat **rising sea levels** and the **melting ice caps** due to decades of overconsumption and pollution. Not to mention all the holes in the **ozone layer**. **In the long run**, it won't make much difference.

Sid: Oh, I hear you. We need to develop more **clean energy** sources. The old **reduce, reuse and recycle** thing isn't good enough. We need **systemic change**.

Drew: I **totally agree** with you. Global warming will lead to humanity's **ultimate** demise.

Vocabulary

greenhouse gas emissions: What is released (mainly carbon dioxide) when fossil fuels are burned.

rising sea levels: How the level of the ocean is increasing year after year.

melting ice caps: There is less ice at the North and South poles because they are melting due to climate change.

in the long run: Over a long period of time.

ozone layer: A layer in the atmosphere that absorbs the UV rays from the sun.

clean energy: Renewable energy like wind, water, and sun.

reduce, reuse, recycle: A slogan about what people can do to help the environment.

systemic change: Change that happens from the top, usually at the government level.

totally agree: Complete agreement about something.

ultimate: The last or final thing.

Practice

1. We need to do more as a country to reduce _____.

2. We can each do our part to save the environment but _____ is also important.

3. Some people will have to leave their island homes in the next few years because of _____.

4. We can all do more to _____.

5. I _____ with you about this! You don't have to convince me.

6. The holes in the _____ are getting bigger and bigger each year.

7. The _____ downfall of our world will be water scarcity.

8. Polar bears are having a difficult time because of the _____.

9. Changing to an electric car will save money _____.

10. Wind and solar power are examples of _____.

Answers

1. greenhouse gas emissions

2. systemic change

3. rising sea levels

4. reduce, reuse, and recycle

5. totally agree

6. ozone layer

7. ultimate

8. melting ice caps

9. in the long run

10. clean energy

The Boy Who Cried Wolf

Once upon a time, in a small village, there lived a young boy named Sam. Sam was responsible for watching over the village's flock of sheep. One day, feeling a bit mischievous, Sam thought it would be amusing to play a **trick** on the **villagers**.

He climbed to the top of a hill and shouted, "Wolf! Wolf! A big, scary wolf is coming to get our sheep!"

Hearing the boy's cry, the villagers hurriedly grabbed their tools and ran to the hill to help. However, when they reached the top, they found no wolf. Sam couldn't stop laughing at the villagers' puzzled faces.

The next day, Sam decided to play the same prank again. Once more, he cried, "Wolf! Wolf! A **fierce** wolf is **attacking** our sheep!"

Concerned for their flock, the villagers rushed to the hill, only to discover Sam's trick once again. This time, they were not amused, and they scolded Sam for his dishonesty.

A few days later, a real wolf appeared on the outskirts of the village. The frightened sheep bleated loudly, and Sam, genuinely scared this time, screamed, "Wolf! Wolf! A dangerous wolf is here!"

However, the villagers, remembering Sam's previous false alarms, hesitated to believe him. They thought he was playing another trick and chose not to respond. Sadly, the wolf attacked the flock, and some sheep were lost.

Sam realized the consequences of his actions. The villagers, disappointed and saddened, explained the importance of **honesty** and trust. From that day forward, Sam learned that telling the truth was crucial, and he worked hard to regain the villagers' trust. The fable of the boy who cried wolf taught everyone in the village the importance of being truthful, as **credibility** is earned through honest words and actions.

The Moral

The moral of the story is that it's important to tell the truth. If we don't tell the truth, people might not believe us when we need help. Being honest is the right thing to do.

Vocabulary

trick: Deceive or outwit.

villagers: People who live in a village (small town).

attacking: Taking aggressive action.

honesty: The quality of telling the truth.

fierce: intense; aggressive.

credibility: The quality of being trusted and believed.

Comprehension Questions

1. Why did Sam shout "Wolf! Wolf!" the first time?
2. How did the villagers respond to Sam's first and second cries for help?
3. What happened when a real wolf came to the village?
4. What did Sam learn from the villagers' reaction to his pranks?
5. What is the moral of the story?

Answers

1. Sam shouted as a prank to trick the villagers and see their reaction.
2. The villagers rushed to help when Sam shouted about the wolf, but they were disappointed when they found out it was a trick the second time.
3. When a real wolf came, Sam shouted for help, but the villagers didn't believe him because of his earlier false alarms. The wolf attacked the sheep.
4. Sam learned that being honest is important because the villagers didn't believe him when a real wolf came.
5. The moral of the story is that it's crucial to tell the truth because if we lie, people may not trust us when we really need help.

Core Values

Lindsey and Ted are talking about a partnership with Tim, a business associate.

Lindsey: I'd like to talk to you about something.

Ted: Sure, what's up?

Lindsey: I'm **not comfortable with** our partnership with Tim anymore. I know it's **highly profitable** but I don't want to be **associated with** him. It raises questions about what our **core values** are.

Ted: I agree. I think we should **take action** on this **as soon as possible**. I've been having the same doubts. We're not quite **breaking the law** but what we're doing isn't really above board.

Lindsey: Okay, good. I'm happy that we're **on the same page**.

Vocabulary

not comfortable with: Not feeling relaxed about something.

highly profitable: Something that can make a lot of money.

associated with: Connected to.

core values: A person or an organization's most important beliefs.

take action: Do something.

as soon as possible: Quickly, at the first possible opportunity.

breaking the law: Doing something illegal.

on the same page: Agree about something.

Practice

1. I'm _____ going out alone at night.

2. One of our _____ is to care for the environment.

3. I want to finish up this assignment _____.

4. My husband and I are _____ with our budget.

5. Even though it's _____, it takes up too much of my time to continue with it.

6. Let's _____ on this tomorrow morning.

7. I can't believe that jaywalking is considered _____ in this city.

8. I don't want to be _____ that guy. Nothing good will come of it.

Answers

1. not comfortable with

2. core values

3. as soon as possible

4. on the same page

5. highly profitable

6. take action

7. breaking the law

8. associated with

Diving Into Coding

Alex and Emma are talking about new challenges.

Alex: Hey, Emma! What's going on? I've been thinking about **taking on** a new challenge lately.

Emma: Really? What are you thinking of tackling?

Alex: I'm considering **diving into** coding. I've heard it's a great skill to **pick up**.

Emma: That sounds interesting! Have you **looked into** any online courses?

Alex: Yeah, I've checked out a few, but I'm still trying to narrow down the options. I might **sign up for** one and see how it goes.

Emma: Nice! I'm actually trying to **cut down on** social media. It's time-consuming, and I want to focus on more meaningful activities.

Alex: I get that. I've been trying to **cut back on** caffeine lately. It's tough, but I want to reduce my dependence on it.

Emma: Well, good luck with that! By the way, have you thought about **teaming up with** someone for coding sessions?

Alex: Funny you mention that. I'm considering teaming up with a friend who's already into coding. We might set up a regular study group.

Emma: That's a great idea! I'm also planning to **clear out** my old stuff and **give away** things I no longer need.

Alex: Decluttering is always a good idea. I might join you and help out. It's about time we cleaned up our spaces.

Emma: Absolutely! Let's plan a day to **sort through** things and get rid of the unnecessary stuff.

Alex: Sounds like a plan! Let's not **back out of** this and make it happen. It's time for some positive changes.

Emma: Agreed! Let's tackle these challenges together and make the most of our time.

Vocabulary

take on: To accept or commit to a challenge or responsibility.

dive into: To start or engage in something enthusiastically or wholeheartedly.

pick up: To acquire a new skill or habit informally or casually.

look into: To investigate or research a topic or matter.

cut down on: To reduce the amount or frequency of something, usually a habit or consumption.

sign up for: To enroll or register for a course, program, or activity.

team up with: To collaborate or work together with someone as a team.

cut back on: To decrease the amount or intensity of something.

clear out: To organize or remove unnecessary items, often by decluttering a space.

give away: To distribute or donate items to others for free.

sort through: To organize or examine a collection of items systematically.

back out of: To withdraw or fail to follow through on a commitment or plan.

Phrasal Verb Challenge

Fill in the blanks with the appropriate phrasal verbs:

1. Lisa and James decided to _____ the new project together.
2. In order to improve efficiency, Lisa is planning to _____ unnecessary tasks from her schedule.
3. James suggested that Lisa should _____ the upcoming conference for professional development.
4. Lisa wants to _____ her workload by delegating some responsibilities to others.
5. James encouraged Lisa to _____ the benefits of outsourcing for certain project aspects.
6. Lisa is considering whether to _____ a course to acquire additional skills for her role.
7. In an effort to stay organized, Lisa plans to _____ her desk and remove

unnecessary items.

8. James and Lisa are ready to _____ the challenge of streamlining their work processes.

9. Lisa is determined to _____ a new language, starting with basic phrases.

10. James suggested they should _____ the possibility of collaborating with other departments on the project.

Answers

1. take on

2. cut down on

3. sign up for

4. cut back on

5. look into

6. pick up

7. clear out

8. dive into

9. pick up

10. team up with

Comprehension Questions

1. What new challenge is Alex considering taking on?
2. What does Alex mention about online courses?
3. What is Emma trying to cut down on?
4. What habit has Alex been trying to cut back on recently?
5. What suggestion does Emma give to Alex regarding coding sessions?
6. What does Emma plan to do with her old stuff?
7. What positive change do Alex and Emma agree to make together?
8. What does Emma propose in terms of sorting through their things?
9. What does Alex suggest they should not do regarding their plans?
10. What is the overall theme of their conversation?

Answers

1. Alex is considering taking on coding as a new challenge.
2. Alex mentions that he has looked into a few online courses for coding.
3. Emma is trying to cut down on social media usage.
4. Alex has been trying to cut back on caffeine.
5. Emma suggests that Alex should consider teaming up with someone for coding sessions.
6. Emma plans to clear out her old stuff and give away things she no longer needs.
7. They agree to tackle challenges together and make positive changes.
8. Emma proposes planning a day to sort through and get rid of unnecessary stuff.
9. Alex suggests they should not back out of their plans.
10. The overall theme is making positive changes, taking on challenges, and decluttering their lives together.

Idioms #3

Call it a day

Meaning: Stop working. Could be paid work or something like cleaning your house or working in the yard.

Origin: First seen in 1838 to refer to someone leaving work at the end of the workday.

"Tony is thinking about *calling it a day*. Do you think you're done, too?"

"Can we please *call it a day?* I'm so tired and my elbow hurts."

Call the shots

Meaning: The leader of a group who makes decisions.

Origin: Appears to originate from the early 1900s, regarding military marksmanship. An excellent marksman makes good shots and "calls" them too (says where they will go). Also refers to some billiards games where you predict which pocket your ball with go into.

"Please talk to Tina. I don't *call the shots* around here."

"I know you want to *call the shots* but he's your boss and you need to let him do that."

Can't judge a book by its cover

Meaning: To not judge something or someone by their outward appearance alone.

Origin: First appeared in 1944 African journal, "*American Speech*" as "don't judge a book by its binding." It evolved to the current form in 1946.

"I know he may not be the most handsome guy but you *can't* always *judge a book by its cover*. He does have a lot of good features, including a well-paying job."

"I know he's a bit difficult to understand with his accent and he wears the same suit every single day but he is the best professor. You *can't judge a book by its cover*."

Cash cow

Meaning: Something that is a reliable source of income.

Origin: Refers to a female dairy cow that gives birth and produces afterwards. Then, she repeats the cycle again. It requires little effort or labour to produce milk. From the 1970s.

"We need to find a *cash cow*. Our current products just don't have enough profit margin."

"That stock is a *cash cow*! The company keeps increasing their dividends every single year."

Catch some rays

Meaning: Means to go outside in the sun.

Origin: From the 1980s surfer subculture in the USA.

"Let's *catch some rays*! It's finally not raining."

"I want to *catch some rays* this weekend. Are there any good beaches around here?"

Cat got your tongue

Meaning: A saying to someone who is unusually quiet.

Origin: Possibly from Egyptian times, when a person's tongue was cut off and fed to cats if the person had lied or been blasphemous.

"Has the *cat got your tongue*? Why are you so quiet?"

"You're unusually quiet here John. What do you think? Has the *cat got your tongue*?

Catnap

Meaning: A short nap.

Origin: First seen in the 1800s.

"My husband loves taking a *catnap* when he gets home from work."

"Why don't you take a *catnap*? I think you'll feel a lot better."

62

Chew it over

Meaning: To take time to think about something before making a decision.

Origin: Uncertain.

"Can I *chew it over* for a week? I need to talk to my wife about it."

"If you're so unsure about that job offer, ask if you can take a couple of days to *chew it over*. I'm sure the company will agree to that."

Chew the fat

Meaning: To gossip or make friendly small talk.

Origin: From the early 1900s and could refer to sailors chewing on salted beef or pork while complaining about life.

"I enjoyed *chewing the fat* with you. It's been years since we've caught up."

"Keith and I *chewed the fat* after work. That's why I'm late."

Come hell or high water

Meaning: To be determined to accomplish something, no matter the circumstances.

Origin: Of American origin but it's not well understood where it came from. The first reference is from a newspaper in 1882.

"Come hell or high water, I'm going to get this project done on time."

"Come hell or high water, I'm not going to let you go to that party so you can stop asking me."

Come rain or shine

Meaning: Something completed or finished, no matter the circumstances (rain or shine). Can be used literally to talk about the weather, or figuratively.

Origin: Used regularly since the mid-1800s.

"*Come rain or shine*, the soccer game will still happen!"

"I'll always love you, *come rain or shine*."

When Pigs Fly

Jerry and Linda are talking about their kids.

Jerry: My kids are **buttering me up** because they don't want to have to help put up **Christmas lights.**

Linda: You're lucky that you can get some help **once in a while**. My kids never **pitch in** for stuff like that. **When pigs fly**, right?

Jerry: Ah, it's all **smoke and mirrors** at my house usually. My kids **make a show out of** cleaning up after themselves after dinner but their rooms are still like a **pigsty**.

Linda: What have we gotten ourselves into?

Vocabulary

when pigs fly: Something that is very unlikely to happen.

pitch in: To contribute to or help with something.

buttering me up: To flatter or please someone because you want something in return. For example, a child who is extra nice to their parents around Christmas because they want an expensive video game system.

smoke and mirrors: Flashy things that distract from what is real.

Christmas lights: Lights on houses for decoration around Christmas.

once in a while: Sometimes.

make a show out of: To do something in a flashy way.

pigsty: Usually refers to a very messy room or space.

Practice

1. I like to let loose _____.

2. His presentation was all _____. No real substance.

3. My kids love to help me put up _____.

4. We all _____ every Saturday morning to clean up the house.

5. My kid's bedroom is a _____.

6. My mom always used to say, "_____" when I asked her for money!

7. I know when my kids are _____ but I fall for it anyway. Their sweet smiles!

8. I hate that my coworkers always _____ finishing even the smallest task.

Answers

1. once in a while

2. smoke and mirrors

3. Christmas lights

4. pitch in

5. pigsty

6. When pigs fly

7. buttering me up

8. make a show out of

The Rise of Teotihuacán

The ancient city of Teotihuacán, nestled in the highlands of central Mexico, stands as a **testament** to the sophisticated and influential cultures that **flourished** in Mesoamerica centuries before the arrival of the Spanish conquistadors. The rise of Teotihuacán, often referred to as the "City of the Gods," is a captivating narrative that unveils the mysteries surrounding this archaeological **marvel**.

Foundations and Early Settlement

Teotihuacán's origins trace back to the Preclassic period (200 BCE - 200 CE), with evidence of small agricultural communities in the region. However, it wasn't until around 150 BCE that the first monumental structures began to emerge. The builders of Teotihuacán employed **innovative** construction techniques, creating impressive pyramids and structures that laid the foundation for the city's future greatness.

Urban Planning and Architecture

The most striking feature of Teotihuacán is its meticulously planned urban layout. The city covers over 20 square kilometers and is designed on a grid system, with the Avenue of the Dead serving as the central axis. Flanked by majestic pyramids and adorned with residential complexes and temples, this grand avenue reflects a deliberate and organized approach to city planning.

The Pyramid of the Sun, one of Teotihuacán's iconic structures, dominates the skyline. Rising to a height of approximately 75 meters, it stands as one of the largest pyramids in the ancient world. The Pyramid of the Moon, another prominent edifice, complements the grandeur of its counterpart, contributing to the overall symmetry and symbolism embedded in the city's architecture.

Cultural Significance and Influence

Teotihuacán's cultural influence extended far beyond its urban borders. The city became a **melting pot** of diverse Mesoamerican cultures, evident in its art, pottery, and murals. The famous "Mural of the Feathered Serpent" in the Temple of the Feathered Serpent (also known as the Temple of the Plumed Serpent) showcases intricate details and symbolic representations, offering insights into the cosmological beliefs and rituals of Teotihuacán's inhabitants.

The influence of Teotihuacán reached distant regions, as trade networks connected the city with other Mesoamerican civilizations. Artifacts discovered at archaeological sites across Mexico attest to the widespread impact of Teotihuacán's cultural and economic prowess.

Demography and Social Structure

Estimates suggest that at its zenith, Teotihuacán was home to a population ranging from 100,000 to 200,000 inhabitants, making it one of the most populous cities of its time. The demographic diversity is evident in the city's housing structures, which include apartment complexes and multi-story buildings. The social organization of Teotihuacán remains a subject of scholarly inquiry, with evidence suggesting a hierarchical structure led by a ruling elite.

Collapse and Theories of Decline

The decline of Teotihuacán is as enigmatic as its rise. Around 600 CE, the city underwent a series of transformations, marked by widespread destruction and abandonment. The reasons behind Teotihuacán's collapse remain speculative, with scholars proposing various theories, including internal unrest, social upheaval, environmental factors, or a combination of these elements.

One prevailing theory suggests that internal conflicts or external invasions might have led to the downfall of the once-thriving metropolis. The intentional destruction of key structures, such as the Feathered Serpent Pyramid, has fueled speculation about violent social unrest or ideological clashes.

Another perspective points to environmental factors, including drought or volcanic activity, disrupting agricultural practices and leading to resource scarcity. These environmental challenges could have triggered social instability and ultimately contributed to the city's abandonment.

Legacy and Archaeological Exploration

Despite its decline, Teotihuacán left an enduring legacy. The Aztecs, who arrived in the region centuries after Teotihuacán's collapse, regarded the city as a sacred site associated with the gods. They named it Teotihuacán, meaning "the place where the gods were created" in Nahuatl, the Aztec language.

Archaeological exploration of Teotihuacán began in the 19th century and continues to the present day. Excavations have unearthed residential areas, marketplaces, and ceremonial complexes, providing invaluable insights into the daily life, religious practices, and economic activities of the city's inhabitants.

Conclusion

The rise of Teotihuacán remains a compelling chapter in the annals of Mesoamerican history. This once-thriving metropolis, with its awe-inspiring architecture and cultural richness, continues to captivate the imagination of scholars and visitors alike. As researchers delve deeper into the mysteries of Teotihuacán, the city's legacy endures not only in the stones and structures that stand testament to its past glory but also in the ongoing quest to understand the complexities of this ancient marvel and the civilizations that called it home.

Vocabulary

archaeological: Relating to the study of past human societies and cultures through the excavation and analysis of artifacts, structures, and other physical remains.

cosmological: Pertaining to the study of the universe's origin, structure, and overall order, often involving religious or cultural beliefs about the cosmos.

hierarchical: Arranged in a system of levels or ranks, where each level is subordinate to the one above it, reflecting a structured and organized order.

symmetry: The quality of being made up of exactly similar parts facing each other or around an axis, creating balance and proportion in design or structure.

enigmatic: Mysterious, puzzling, or difficult to understand, often referring to something that arouses curiosity or intrigue due to its unclear nature.

zenith: The highest point or culmination, representing the peak or apex of a process, achievement, or celestial body's path in the sky.

ceremonial: Relating to formal or ritualistic observances, often associated with religious, cultural, or symbolic events.

annals: Historical records or accounts, often chronicling events in chronological order, providing a written narrative of significant occurrences over time.

Vocabulary Challenge

1. Testament, in the first paragraph is closest in meaning to:
    a) evidence
    b) related to the Bible
    c) a will
    d) a fact

2. Flourished, in the first paragraph is closest in meaning to:

   a) got smaller

   b) waving arms

   c) developed well

   d) moved around

3. Marvel, in the first paragraph is closest in meaning to:

   a) filled with anger

   b) filled with excitement

   c) a disappointing thing

   d) an impressive thing

4. Innovative, in the second paragraph is closest in meaning to:

   a) exciting

   b) well-tested

   c) featuring something new

   d) interesting

5. Melting pot, in the fifth paragraph is closest in meaning to:

   a) a place where people blend together well

   b) a place where people maintain their individual identities

   c) a pot where people make fondue

   d) a place where gold and silver are melted

Answers

   1. a

   2. c

   3. d

   4. c

   5. a

Multiple Choice Questions

1. What is the primary focus of archaeological studies?

   a) Analysis of climate patterns

   b) Exploration of ancient civilizations

   c) Observation of celestial bodies

   d) Examination of genetic codes

2. Which term refers to a structured system with levels or ranks, where each level is subordinate to the one above it?

   a) Symmetry

   b) Hierarchical

   c) Cosmological

   d) Archaeological

3. What does the term "cosmological" relate to in the context of ancient cultures?

   a) Urban planning

   b) Celestial bodies

   c) Agricultural practices

   d) Social hierarchies

4. In the context of architecture, what does "symmetry" refer to?

   a) A mysterious design

   b) Balanced proportions

   c) Formal rituals

   d) Skilled craftsmanship

5. Which word describes something that is mysterious and difficult to understand?

a) Prowess

b) Annals

c) Enigmatic

d) Zenith

6. What does the term "zenith" signify in the context of a celestial body's path?

a) The lowest point

b) The highest point

c) A circular path

d) The starting point

7. What is prowess in the context of a person's abilities?

a) A ceremonial practice

b) Exceptional skill or ability

c) Historical records

d) Urban planning

8. Which term refers to structured records chronicling events in chronological order?

a) Prowess

b) Annals

c) Symmetry

d) Zenith

9. What does the term "ceremonial" typically relate to?

a) Skilled craftsmanship

b) Ritualistic observances

c) Hierarchical structures

d) Celestial bodies

10. What is the primary focus of the field of archaeology?

   a) Exploration of contemporary societies

   b) Analysis of living organisms

   c) Examination of ancient artifacts and structures

   d) Observation of astronomical phenomena

Answers

   1. b
   2. b
   3. b
   4. d
   5. c
   6. b
   7. b
   8. b
   9. b
   10. c

Asking for Clarification

Harper is asking for clarification from Logan.

Harper: Just so I'm clear on this: you're asking me to **scale back** production on Model 1234?

Logan: Yes, correct. Fuel prices are **skyrocketing** and there isn't as much demand for things that aren't fuel-efficient. Put it on the **backburner** for now.

Harper: Is this the plan **for the long haul**?

Logan: **Pretty much** as long as fuel prices remain at current levels and we're **in the red**. We're **feeling the pinch** with our expansion into Canada and we just don't have **money to burn** like we did a few years ago.

Harper: Okay, I got it. I'll let my team know.

Vocabulary

scale back: Reduce something.

skyrocketing: Increasing rapidly

backburner: Leave something for now and deal with it later.

for the long haul: For the long term.

pretty much: Almost 100% certain.

in the red: Losing money.

feeling the pinch: Experiencing financial difficulties.

money to burn: Extra money to spend freely.

Practice

1. Look at that new car he bought. He must have _____.

2. My company is in it _____.

3. I'm worried about this project that's now running _____.

4. We're _____ with Covid-19.

5. I _____ only want to know where I stand with this company.

6. Let's put this on the _____ until the economy recovers.

7. Fuel prices are _____ these days with the shortages.

8. Let's _____ production until the new model comes out.

Answers

1. money to burn

2. for the long haul

3. in the red

4. feeling the pinch

5. pretty much

6. backburner

7. skyrocketing

8. scale back

The Fox and the Crow

In a serene forest, a **clever** fox and an **curious** crow lived amongst the trees. One day, the crow discovered a delectable piece of cheese and perched on a high branch to savor its find.

Observing the crow from a distance, the fox **hatched** a **cunning** plan. Approaching the crow with a smile, the fox spoke, "Greetings, noble crow! I've heard tales of your magnificent singing. Would you do me the honor of gracing the forest with your melodious voice?"

The crow, flattered by the fox's praise, eagerly opened its **beak** to sing. However, as the beautiful notes filled the air, the piece of cheese slipped from the crow's beak and fell to the ground below.

Seizing the opportunity, the fox swiftly grabbed the cheese, expressing gratitude, "Thank you, gracious crow! Your singing is as splendid as rumored." With the stolen prize in its jaws, the fox made a quick escape, leaving the crow bewildered and without its cherished cheese.

The moral of the story imparts a lesson about the danger of being easily swayed by **flattery**. The fox used charming words to deceive the crow and snatch the prize, emphasizing the importance of discernment and not letting sweet words cloud one's judgment.

The Moral

The moral of the story is to be careful and not believe everything people say, especially if they want something from you. It teaches us to be cautious and not let flattery or kind words cloud our judgment.

Vocabulary

beak: The nose of a bird.

clever: Smart; intelligent.

curious: Eager to know or learn about something.

flattery: Excessive praise.

hatched: Came up with.

cunning: Tricky; deceitful.

Comprehension Questions

1. Why did the fox approach the crow?
2. What did the fox compliment the crow on?
3. What did the crow do when the fox asked it to sing?
4. What happened while the crow was singing?
5. How did the fox get the cheese?

Answers

1. The fox approached the crow because it saw the crow with a piece of cheese and wanted to find a way to get it.
2. The fox complimented the crow on being a magnificent bird and suggested that it had heard the crow's singing was extraordinary.
3. The crow, flattered by the fox's words, opened its beak to sing.
4. While the crow was singing, the piece of cheese fell from its beak to the ground below.
5. The sly fox took advantage of the crow's singing, grabbed the fallen cheese, and thanked the crow before running away.

Get Into Trouble

Ian is talking to Ted about his many problems on the weekend.

Ted: Hey Ian, how was your weekend?

Ian: Oh, I **got into trouble** again! I got a **parking ticket, got lost** while hiking and then maybe got **food poisoning**.

Ted: Oh wow. That sounds terrible. You always have interesting stories though, right?

Ian: I'm **envious of** your life. It seems much calmer.

Ted: Well, it's **not all rainbows and unicorns**. I **asked somebody out** but she rejected me. I'm thinking about **giving up** on dating altogether.

Ian: Hang in there my friend. There are **plenty of fish in the sea**.

Vocabulary

got into trouble: Had some problems happen.

parking ticket: A fine you have to pay for parking illegally.

got lost: Didn't know where you were.

food poisoning: Getting sick from something that you ate.

envious of: Jealous of.

not all rainbows and unicorns: Real life isn't as good as it appears to others.

asked somebody out: Asked someone if they wanted to go on a date.

giving up: Stop trying.

plenty of fish in the sea: There are many eligible people to date.

Practice

1. He _____ out hiking because he didn't have any extra clothes or food and then he got lost.

2. When was the last time you _____? Maybe that's why you don't have a girlfriend!

3. I _____ all the time when I was visiting Seoul. It's such a big city!

4. Do you think that maybe it's _____? Why don't you go to the ER?

5. I'm _____ Joe. He always seems to have so many ladies to go on dates with.

6. I'm thinking about _____ scuba diving. It's such an expensive hobby.

7. Things are not always as they appear. My life is _____.

8. I know you're sad but there are _____.

9. If you don't pay your _____ on time, the fine doubles after a month.

Answers

1. got into trouble

2. asked somebody out

3. got lost

4. food poisoning

5. envious of

6. giving up

7. not all rainbows and unicorns

8. plenty of fish in the sea

9. parking ticket

At the Coffee Shop

Lisa and James meet at a bustling coffee shop during a work break.

Lisa: James, I've been swamped with projects lately. Let's **catch up** and discuss the new assignment.

James: Absolutely, Lisa. I've been meaning to touch base with you. Grab a table, and we can **go over** the details.

Lisa: I'm really struggling to **keep up** with the workload. I need to **figure out** a way to **cut down on** the extra tasks.

James: I get it. We should brainstorm some strategies to streamline the process. How about delegating some responsibilities?

Lisa: Good idea. I've been **putting off** that task, but it's time to start **handing over** some of the workload.

James: Speaking of which, have you considered outsourcing some aspects of the project? It could **free up** a lot of your time.

Lisa: I haven't thought about that. It's worth **looking into**. I'll explore the option and see if it makes sense for us. By the way, have you heard about the upcoming conference? We should **sign up** and stay ahead in our field.

James: I'm all for it. Let's register and make sure we don't miss out on any valuable insights.

(As they finish their coffee)

Lisa: Thanks for meeting up, James. I needed this chat to clear my head and strategize.

James: Anytime, Lisa. We make a great team, and I'm sure we'll tackle these challenges together.

Vocabulary

catch up: To reconnect or exchange information with someone after a period of separation.

go over: Consider or examine.

keep up: Move at the same rate as other people.

figure out: Solve a problem.

cut down on: Reduce.

put off: Delay.

hand over: Give responsibility to someone else.

free up: Make available for sure.

look into: Investigate something.

sign up: Commit oneself to something.

Phrasal Verb Challenge

Fill in the blanks with the appropriate phrasal verb:

1. After a long trip, Susan wanted to _____ with her friends and hear about their latest news.

2. Before making a decision, it's crucial to thoroughly _____ all the details and options available.

3. If you want to _____ with the competition, you'll need to stay updated on the latest industry trends.

4. Unable to _____ the complex puzzle, Amy asked her friend for assistance.

5. To improve your health, it's advisable to _____ the consumption of sugary beverages.

6. Due to unforeseen circumstances, the project manager had to _____ the meeting to next week.

7. The overwhelmed CEO decided to _____ some of his responsibilities to focus on core tasks.

8. Clearing unnecessary files will _____ space on your computer for better performance.

9. The detective promised to _____ the mysterious disappearance and get to the bottom of it.

10. Interested participants can _____ for the workshop online.

Answers

1. catch up
2. go over
3. keep up
4. figure out
5. cut down on
6. put off
7. hand over
8. free up
9. look into
10. sign up

Comprehension Questions

1. Where do Lisa and James meet for a catch-up?
2. What is Lisa's current workload situation?
3. What does James suggest as a strategy to help Lisa with her workload?
4. What does Lisa agree to consider as part of streamlining her tasks?
5. What does James propose as a proactive step to stay ahead in their field?
6. Why does Lisa think outsourcing could be beneficial?
7. What does Lisa say about her approach to a specific task?
8. How does James describe their teamwork?
9. What does James acknowledge about Lisa's current situation?
10. What is the tone of the conversation between Lisa and James?

Answers

1. Lisa and James meet at a bustling coffee shop.

2. Lisa mentions that she has been swamped with projects.

3. James suggests delegating some responsibilities to lighten Lisa's workload.

4. Lisa agrees to consider outsourcing some aspects of the project.

5. James suggests signing up for an upcoming conference to stay ahead in their field.

6. Lisa thinks outsourcing could free up a lot of her time and help streamline the process.

7. Lisa mentions that she has been putting off the task of delegating responsibilities.

8. James mentions, "We make a great team."

9. James acknowledges that Lisa is struggling with her workload.

10. The tone of the conversation is supportive and collaborative.

Noise Pollution

Kathleen and Kenny are talking about living in Busan.

Kathleen: Kenny! You lived in Busan, South Korea? I've always wanted to go there. What's it like? I've heard that it's a beautiful **coastal city**.

Kenny: Well, there's a lot of **noise pollution** and **light pollution**. It's the second biggest city in Korea. And **traffic jams** too during **rush hour**.

Kathleen: It sounds terrible.

Kenny: Oh no, it's amazing! I love Nampo-Dong, which has lots of **street food** and **street vendors** plus **trendy cafes**. It's perfect for a date.

Kathleen: What else?

Kenny: Well, there's no real **downtown core** or **main square** but there are six beaches within **city limits**. Most people just hang out there, especially in the summertime.

Vocabulary

coastal city: A city next to the ocean.

noise pollution: Ambient noise in a city. For example, cars honking.

light pollution: Light from signs and cars that you can see inside your house at night.

traffic jams: Lots of cars on the road which makes progress slower than normal.

rush hour: The busiest times to drive, usually because of people going to work and coming home from work.

street food: Food from an outside stall.

street vendors: People selling things at an outside stall.

trendy cafes: Coffee shops that are fashionable and hip.

downtown core: The area in a city with lots of tall buildings; an important place of business.

main square: The most important public courtyard in a city.

city limits: The outer edge of the city, including suburbs. Not just the downtown core.

Practice

1. I love to buy Christmas presents from _____. There are lots of interesting things.

2. Vancouver is the best _____ in Canada.

3. Within the _____, you can find three beaches and countless parks.

4. Go after 9:30 am to avoid _____.

5. Where's the _____? I'd love to spend some time there and people watch.

6. The best _____ in Korea? Honestly, I can't choose. There are many delicious things.

7. The _____ in Edmonton is famous for being boring at night.

8. _____ makes it difficult for me to sleep at night even though I have blackout curtains.

9. My boyfriend loves to spend time at _____ on weekends. I think they're expensive!

10. During _____, it takes twice as long to get home.

11. The _____ is terrible here. I have to wear earplugs to sleep at night.

Answers

1. street vendors

2. coastal city

3. city limits

4. traffic jams

5. main square

6. street food

7. downtown core

8. light pollution

9. trendy cafes

10. rush hour

11. noise pollution

Darwin's Theory of Evolution

Charles Darwin's Theory of Evolution, presented in his **seminal** work "On the Origin of Species" in 1859, stands as a pivotal **milestone** in the history of biology. This groundbreaking theory reshaped our comprehension of life's origins and diversification, challenging prevailing beliefs and setting the stage for a unified framework in the biological sciences.

Natural Selection: The Engine of Evolution

At the core of Darwin's theory is the concept of natural selection, a mechanism that propels the gradual adaptation of species to their environment. Darwin observed the existence of variation in traits within populations and proposed that this diversity plays a crucial role in a species' ability to survive and reproduce. Natural selection acts as a selective force, favoring traits that **confer** advantages in the struggle for existence and gradually leading to the evolution of species over time.

Malthusian Influence: Population Dynamics in Nature

Darwin drew inspiration from the work of economist Thomas Malthus, who **posited** that human populations grow exponentially, leading to competition for limited resources. Darwin applied this principle to the natural world, suggesting that organisms, like human populations, face a constant struggle for existence. This struggle serves as the **crucible** in which natural selection operates, favoring traits that enhance an individual's chances of survival and reproduction.

Observations from the HMS Beagle: A Journey into Diversity

Darwin's voyage on the HMS Beagle provided him with a wealth of firsthand observations, particularly in the Galápagos Islands. These observations showcased variations in species adapted to different ecological niches, offering tangible evidence for the operation of natural selection. Additionally, his studies of domesticated plants and animals illuminated patterns of change over time, contributing to the formulation of his evolutionary theory.

Challenging Prevailing Beliefs: The Evolution-Religion Nexus

Darwin's theory challenged deeply rooted religious beliefs that advocated a fixed and unchanging creation. The concept of evolution by natural selection presented a dynamic and gradual process that contradicted traditional views. This clash between science and religious orthodoxy ignited controversy and resistance, marking a significant turning point in the relationship between science and faith.

Empirical Support and Interdisciplinary Corroboration

Over time, Darwin's theory garnered empirical support from diverse scientific disciplines. Fossil records provided evidence of transitional forms, while comparative anatomy and molecular biology revealed homologous structures and common ancestry among different organisms. Advances in genetics in the 20th century further solidified the molecular basis for evolutionary change.

Legacy and Beyond: Darwin's Lasting Impact

Darwin's Theory of Evolution transcended the realm of biology, sparking debates in ethics, philosophy, and theology. It influenced discussions on human nature, morality, and humanity's place in the natural world. As we unravel the mysteries of biology, Darwin's insights endure as a guiding beacon, emphasizing the dynamic and ever-evolving nature of life's interconnected tapestry.

Vocabulary

evolution: The process of gradual change over time, especially the development of species through natural selection.

natural selection: The mechanism by which certain traits within a population are favored over others, leading to the increased likelihood of those traits being passed on to future generations.

adaptation: The adjustment or modification of an organism's features or behaviors to suit its environment, enhancing its chances of survival and reproduction.

variation: Differences or diversity in traits observed among individuals within a population of organisms.

species: A group of organisms that share common characteristics and can interbreed to produce fertile offspring.

fossil records: Preserved remains or traces of ancient organisms found in rocks, providing insights into the history of life on Earth.

homologous structures: Similar anatomical structures found in different species, indicating a common evolutionary origin.

Malthusian: Relating to the ideas of Thomas Malthus, particularly the theory that population growth can outpace the availability of resources, leading to competition and natural selection.

empirical: Based on observation, experience, or evidence from the real world rather than theory or speculation.

paradigm shift: A fundamental change in a scientific theory or approach that results in a new way of understanding or explaining phenomena.

Vocabulary Challenge

1. Seminal, in the first paragraph is closest in meaning to:
   a) something related to plants
   b) something that strongly influences other things
   c) the first
   d) something new

2. Milestone, in the first paragraph is closest in meaning to:

   a) a stone that marks a mile in distance

   b) a method of punishment

   c) something significant

   d) the foundation of a building

3. Confer, in the second paragraph is closest in meaning to:

   a) have a discussion

   b) informal talk with friends

   c) bestow

   d) move

4. Posited, in the third paragraph is closest in meaning to:

   a) put forward as an argument

   b) factually proved

   c) put into position

   d) put money into the bank

5. Crucible, in the third paragraph is closest in meaning to:

   a) a glass or ceramic container

   b) a metal container

   c) a science laboratory

   d) a place where elements interact

Answers

   1. b

   2. c

   3. c

   4. a

   5. d

89

Multiple Choice Questions

1. What is the central concept of Darwin's Theory of Evolution?

   a) Genetic engineering

   b) Natural selection

   c) Artificial selection

   d) Genetic drift

2. Which scientist's work on population dynamics influenced Darwin's thinking about competition for resources?

   a) Albert Einstein

   b) Gregor Mendel

   c) Thomas Malthus

   d) Louis Pasteur

3. What term describes the gradual modification of an organism's features to suit its environment?

   a) Mutation

   b) Adaptation

   c) Hybridization

   d) Evolution

4. In the context of evolution, what does the term "variation" refer to?

   a) Differences in traits among individuals within a population

   b) Geographic distribution of a species

   c) The rate of mutation in a population

   d) The process of natural selection

5. What is the primary source of evidence supporting the theory of evolution from a historical perspective?

    a) Genetic sequencing

    b) Homologous structures

    c) Paleontological fossil records

    d) Artificial selection experiments

6. Which term describes structures in different species that share a common evolutionary origin?

    a) Analogous structures

    b) Homologous structures

    c) Vestigial structures

    d) Mutant structures

7. What was the groundbreaking work by Charles Darwin where he first presented his theory of evolution?

    a) Principles of Geology

    b) The Descent of Man

    c) The Voyage of the Beagle

    d) On the Origin of Species

8. Which term describes the process by which certain traits become more or less common in a population over generations due to random events?

    a) Genetic engineering

    b) Genetic drift

    c) Natural selection

    d) Artificial selection

9. In the context of evolution, what is the term for a group of organisms that can interbreed and produce fertile offspring?

a) Genus

b) Order

c) Family

d) Species

10. What does the term "paradigm shift" mean in the scientific context?

a) A fundamental change in scientific theory or approach

b) A temporary shift in climate patterns

c) A sudden mutation in a population

d) The introduction of a new species to an ecosystem

Answers

1. b
2. c
3. b
4. a
5. c
6. b
7. d
8. b
9. d
10. a

Talking about a Customer

Emma is talking to Oliver about one of their customers.

Emma: Hey, so I was just talking to Noah and it looks like they won't renew the contract. It's a bit **up in the air** but I think they want to **sever ties** with us.

Oliver: To me, **the writing is on the wall**. They haven't been happy for months now.

Emma: Not to **throw someone under the bus** but the **elephant in the room** is Mia's performance as their account manager. It's just not good enough.

Oliver: I think you've **hit the nail on the head**. She's already **in the dog house** with that other account she manages.

Emma: She's **all talk**. It's time she **puts her money where her mouth is**.

Oliver: I'd love to go behind her back and **blow the whistle** on this but I don't want to draw attention to myself.

Vocabulary

up in the air: Not decided yet.

sever ties: To stop a relationship.

the writing is on the wall: It's obvious to everyone.

throw someone under the bus: To blame someone for something.

the elephant in the room: The obvious thing that nobody is talking about.

hit the nail on the head: See the problem clearly.

in the dog house: In trouble.

all talk: Good at talking but their actions don't reflect this.

puts her money where her mouth is: Her actions need to reflect her words.

blow the whistle: To disclose true information that might be harmful to someone.

Practice

1. Honestly, I just think he should _____ on his company. They're doing some terrible things.

2. I'm _____ with my kids if I get home too late from work.

3. I think we need to _____ with that contractor.

4. Why is nobody talking about _____?

5. It's time for her to _____ and do some work.

6. He's _____ but no action.

7. I hate that we have to _____ for this.

8. You've made a good point and _____ exactly.

9. Don't you think that _____? I'm going to get fired.

10. I don't think she's made the decision yet. It's still _____.

Answers

1. blow the whistle

2. in the dog house

3. sever ties

4. the elephant in the room

5. put her money where her mouth is

6. all talk

7. throw someone under the bus

8. hit the nail on the head

9. the writing is on the wall

10. up in the air

A Council of Mice

Once upon a time in a quiet meadow, there lived a **community** of mice. The mice were small but wise, and they had a leader named Whiskerington. One day, a group of mice noticed that the village cat, known as Whiskers, was catching more and more mice every day. The mice were frightened and didn't know what to do.

Feeling the need for a solution, the mice gathered for a **council** to discuss their predicament. Whiskerington, with his long whiskers and wise eyes, **presided** over the meeting.

A brave mouse named Squeaky spoke up first, "We must find a way to **outsmart** Whiskers and avoid being caught. Perhaps we can create a plan to **alert** each other when Whiskers is nearby."

Another mouse named Swift suggested, "What if we build safe **hiding spots** where we can quickly retreat if Whiskers comes too close?"

After much discussion, the council of mice decided to implement both ideas. They created a system of signals to warn each other about the cat's presence and built small, secure hiding places throughout the meadow. As days passed, the plan worked well, and the mice felt safer. Whiskers, no longer able to catch mice easily, grew frustrated and eventually gave up.

The moral of the story is that by working together and using their intelligence, the mice were able to overcome a common threat. It teaches us that unity and cleverness can overcome challenges, even when faced with a formidable opponent.

The Moral

The moral of the story is that when we work together and use our brains, we can solve problems and stay safe, even from something scary like a cat. Teamwork and clever thinking help us overcome challenges.

Vocabulary

hiding spots: Places where someone or something can't be found.

community: Group of people or animals.

council: Leaders or a group.

presided: Held a high position in a meeting.

outsmart: Defeat.

alert: Notify; tell.

Comprehension Questions

1. What was the problem that the mice faced in the story?
2. Who was the leader of the mice?
3. What were the two ideas the mice decided to use to stay safe from Whiskers?
4. Did the plan of the mice work against Whiskers? How?
5. What does the story teach us about solving problems?

Answers

1. The mice faced a problem of being caught by a cat named Whiskers.
2. Whiskerington was the leader of the mice.
3. The mice decided to warn each other when Whiskers was close and to build safe hiding spots.
4. Yes, the plan worked. By warning each other and having safe hiding spots, Whiskers couldn't catch the mice anymore.
5. The story teaches us that working together and using our brains can help us solve problems and stay safe.

Knowledge-Based Economy

A TA is discussing an issue in an Economics tutorial.

Canada is now a **knowledge-based economy**. Workers who ignore that do so at their own **peril**. Most of the **manufacturing** jobs, and especially the good **union** jobs, have now been **outsourced** to places with cheaper labour like India or China. Those who lack the skills to operate in a digital world risk being left out of the **job market** altogether.

One option is **retraining**. However, that can be quite difficult with older workers who are not that familiar with using computers. It can be an **uphill battle**. There are some **alternatives** as well as to what to do for these workers who get **laid off** from manufacturing jobs. Has anyone seen any approaches mentioned in the news lately? Let's talk about some of the new programs.

Vocabulary

knowledge-based economy: A kind of economy where information or intellectual skills are most important.

peril: Risk.

manufacturing: Making something.

union: An organization that negotiates for and protects a group of workers from employers.

outsourced: Work that is sent to another country, company, etc.

job market: Where employees look for jobs and employers look for workers.

retraining: Learning new skills for a different kind of job than currently doing.

uphill battle: Describes something very difficult to do or achieve.

alternatives: Other options.

laid off: A worker is temporarily or permanently stopped from working because of a situation out of their control.

Practice

1. Older people often have a difficult time adapting to a _____.

2. The _____ is great for employees these days. Wages keep going up.

3. Good _____ jobs with benefits are difficult to find in Europe these days.

4. Learning computer skills later in life is an _____ for some people.

5. My company _____ customer service to India last year.

6. We'll have to switch to digital records soon. If we don't, it's at our own _____.

7. My wife got _____ when her company went out of business.

8. I might do some _____ and learn how to become a car mechanic.

9. Why don't you consider the _____ before making a decision? You're overlooking some of them.

10. The _____ dues (fees) are quite high but it's maybe worth it? The union did negotiate a good contract for us last year.

Answers

1. knowledge-based economy

2. job market

3. manufacturing

4. uphill battle

5. outsourced

6. peril

7. laid off

8. retraining

9. alternatives

10. union

Swamped with Work

Mark is talking about how busy he is at work.

Emily: Hey Mark! Long time no see. What's going on with you?

Mark: Hey Emily! I've been **swamped with** work lately, but I'm trying to **break down** this complex project. I need to finish it up by the end of the week.

Emily: I get that. How do you plan to tackle it?

Mark: Well, I'm going to start by breaking it up into smaller tasks. I'll **chip away at** each one and hopefully finish them off one by one.

Emily: Smart move! If you need any help, feel free to reach out. I can **pitch in** with some of the easier tasks.

Mark: Thanks, Emily! I might take you up on that offer. I also need to **catch up on** emails and follow up with clients. It's been piling up.

Emily: Oh, I totally get it. You should set aside some time each day to **knock out** those emails. Don't let them build up too much.

Mark: True, I need to **sort through** them and get back to people. I also have to put together a presentation for the upcoming meeting. I'm not looking forward to it.

Emily: No worries! We can brainstorm some ideas and put the presentation together. We'll have it **nailed down** in no time.

Mark: That sounds like a plan. Let's **meet up** later this week to go over everything. I appreciate the support, Emily!

Vocabulary

swamped with: Overwhelmed or burdened by, as in being swamped with work.

break down: To analyze or divide into smaller parts, in this context, breaking down a complex project into manageable tasks.

chip away at: To make gradual progress by working on a task bit by bit, mentioned in relation to finishing the smaller tasks.

pitch in: To contribute or help, as in offering assistance with some of the easier tasks.

catch up on: To get up to date or complete tasks that have been neglected, as in catching up on emails and following up with clients.

sort through: To organize or arrange by categorizing or selecting, mentioned in relation to sorting through emails.

knock out: To quickly and efficiently complete a task, as mentioned in knocking out emails.

nailed down: To finalize or clarify something, as in finalizing the details of a presentation.

meet up: To come together or arrange a meeting, as in meeting up later in the week to discuss the project.

Phrasal Verb Challenge

Fill in the blanks with the appropriate phrasal verbs:

1. I've been _____ work lately, handling numerous tasks simultaneously.
2. Can you help me _____ this complicated report into smaller sections for a clearer understanding?
3. We need to _____ this project by tackling each aspect steadily.
4. It's a challenging project, but if everyone can _____, we'll finish it more efficiently.
5. This weekend, I plan to _____ my emails and make sure I respond to all the pending messages.
6. Before starting the new project, it's crucial to _____ the existing data and documents.
7. We have a tight deadline, so let's work together and _____ these tasks swiftly.
8. Once we have _____ the details, we can proceed with the final preparations for the presentation.
9. Let's _____ later this week to discuss our progress and address any concerns.
10. Despite the workload, we will successfully _____ the challenges.

Answers

1. swamped with
2. break down
3. chip away at
4. pitch in
5. catch up on
6. sort through
7. knock out
8. nailed down
9. meet up
10. get through

Comprehension Questions

1. Why does Mark feel swamped with work lately?
2. How does Mark plan to approach his complex project?
3. In what way does Emily offer to help Mark with his workload?
4. What tasks does Mark need to catch up on?
5. What does Emily propose they do to finalize the presentation?
6. According to Emily, what should Mark set aside time for?
7. How does Mark intend to make progress on his project?
8. What does Emily suggest Mark do with his emails?
9. Why does Mark need to put together a presentation?
10. When and why do Mark and Emily plan to meet up later in the week?

Answers

1. Mark feels swamped with work because he has a lot of tasks to complete.

2. Mark plans to break down his complex project into smaller tasks.

3. Emily offers to pitch in and help Mark with some of the easier tasks.

4. Mark needs to catch up on emails and follow up with clients.

5. Emily suggests they brainstorm ideas together to nail down the presentation.

6. Emily suggests Mark should set aside some time each day to knock out his emails.

7. Mark plans to chip away at his project by working on it bit by bit.

8. Emily suggests Mark should sort through his emails to stay organized.

9. Mark needs to put together a presentation for an upcoming meeting.

10. Mark and Emily plan to meet up later in the week to discuss their progress on the project.

Feeling Under the Weather

Jerry is talking to his friend Linda about being sick.

Jerry: I know, I know. My mom used to tell me to not be such a **couch potato** and that **an apple a day keeps the doctor away**. I wish that I'd listened to her! I'm feeling **worse for wear**.

Linda: Keep your chin up! I know you're **feeling under the weather** but **this too shall pass**.

Jerry: Thanks Linda, I appreciate you **checking in on** me every day.

Linda: It's the least I can do. You've helped me with so many things over the years. Just don't **kick the bucket** on me, okay?

Vocabulary

feeling under the weather: Not feeling well; feeling sick.

keep your chin up: Telling something to stay strong. Encouraging someone in a tough situation.

couch potato: Someone who spends lots of time on the couch watching TV or movies or playing video games. Not active.

an apple a day keeps the doctor away: Eating healthy keeps you from getting sick.

this too shall pass: A bad period of time that will eventually end.

checking in on: To see how someone is doing.

it's the least I can do: No problem; it's a small thing, usually when you feel like you should do more.

worse for wear: Feeling worn out or tired.

kick the bucket: Die.

Practice

1. My dad keeps phoning and _____ me. It's almost too much!

2. I keep nagging my son to get active because he's such a _____.

3. I called in sick because I was feeling a bit _____.

4. My mom is great at telling people to _____ when something bad happens.

5. I'm convinced that the saying, "_____" really does work!

6. My son has been pretty down lately but I told him that, "_____."

7. Lunch is on me. _____, seeing as you've been making me meals all week.

8. I'm _____ after being in the hospital for more than a week. It was impossible to sleep there.

9. I hope that I don't _____ before I'm 80 but I'm nervous about how much I smoke!

Answers

1. checking in on

2. couch potato

3. under the weather

4. keep your chin up

5. An apple a day keeps the doctor away

6. This too shall pass

7. It's the least I can do

8. worse for wear

9. kick the bucket

The Nile River

The Nile River, often hailed as the **lifeblood** of northeastern Africa, weaves through the tapestry of the continent, leaving an indelible mark on the landscapes it traverses. Spanning approximately 6,650 kilometers (4,130 miles), the Nile stands as the longest river in the world, an ancient watercourse that has profoundly shaped the histories, cultures, and ecosystems of the diverse nations it touches. This majestic river holds a mystique that transcends geographical boundaries, embodying both the **cradle** of ancient civilizations and a contemporary source of vitality for the millions who depend on its waters.

Originating in the Heart of Africa

The Nile's journey begins deep in the heart of Africa, where its two main tributaries, the White Nile and the Blue Nile, converge in Khartoum, Sudan. The White Nile, originating from Lake Victoria, and the Blue Nile, rising from Lake Tana in Ethiopia, join forces to create the mighty Nile River, a confluence that marks the commencement of its extraordinary **odyssey**. From this point onward, the river winds its way northward, sculpting landscapes and nurturing a myriad of life forms along its course.

Historical Significance

The Nile is not merely a geographical feature; it is a historical tapestry woven into the narratives of ancient civilizations. Egypt, often regarded as the gift of the Nile, owes its prosperity to the annual flooding of the riverbanks, a natural phenomenon that **replenished** the soil with nutrient-rich sediments, fostering fertile lands along the Nile Delta. The ancient Egyptians recognized the cyclical nature of the river's flooding and developed sophisticated agricultural practices that allowed their civilization to thrive for millennia.

Beyond Egypt, the Nile also played a **pivotal** role in the development of Nubian and Sudanese civilizations. The river served as a lifeline for trade, communication, and sustenance, connecting communities along its banks and facilitating cultural exchanges that enriched the diverse tapestry of the region.

Ecosystem Diversity

The Nile River basin encompasses a remarkable diversity of ecosystems, ranging from dense tropical rainforests in its upper reaches to arid deserts in the north. This ecological richness has made the Nile a haven for a wide array of plant and animal species, many of which are endemic to the region. The river supports a wealth of biodiversity, from the iconic Nile crocodile and the elusive manatee to a plethora of bird species that thrive along its shores.

Contemporary Importance

In the 21st century, the Nile remains an indispensable resource for the countries through which it flows. The river serves as a source of water for agriculture, industry, and domestic use, sustaining the livelihoods of millions. However, the allocation and management of the Nile's waters have also been a source of contention among the riparian states, highlighting the complex geopolitical dynamics intertwined with this vital waterway.

As the Nile continues to flow through the annals of time, its significance persists, evolving to meet the needs of a changing world. The river's storied past, ecological diversity, and contemporary importance underscore its status as not just a geographic feature but a cultural, historical, and economic force that binds the destinies of the nations it touches. In the following exploration, we will delve deeper into the various facets of the Nile, unraveling its mysteries and appreciating its profound impact on the past, present, and future of northeastern Africa.

Vocabulary

confluence: The point at which two rivers or streams meet and flow together.

sediments: Particles of solid material, such as sand or soil, that settle at the bottom of a liquid, often carried by water.

cyclical: Occurring in cycles or repeated patterns.

riparian: Relating to or situated on the banks of a river or other body of water.

endemic: Native to a specific region and found nowhere else.

biodiversity: The variety of plant and animal life in a particular habitat or ecosystem.

geopolitical: Relating to the political and territorial relations between countries.

riparian states: Countries or regions that are located along the banks of a river or other body of water.

fertile: Capable of producing abundant vegetation or crops; rich in nutrients.

annals: Historical records or accounts, often in chronological order, detailing events and developments.

Vocabulary Challenge

1. Lifeblood, in the first paragraph is closest in meaning to:

    a) blood of humans or animals

    b) something large

    c) something unnecessary

    d) something indispensable

2. Cradle, in the first paragraph is closest in meaning to:

    a) move side to side

    b) where a baby sleeps

    c) a place where something begins

    d) where a ship rests out of the water

3. Odyssey, in the second paragraph is closest in meaning to:

a) a long journey

b) a famous book

c) the beginning of something

d) the end of something

4. Replenished, in the third paragraph is closest in meaning to:

a) started over

b) depleted

c) filled something up again

d) took something away

5. Pivotal, in the fourth paragraph is closest in meaning to:

a) what athletes do

b) changing direction

c) somewhat important

d) of crucial importance

Answers

1. d

2. c

3. a

4. c

5. d

Multiple Choice Questions

1. What is the primary source of the Nile River?

   a) Lake Tanganyika

   b) Lake Victoria

   c) Lake Malawi

   d) Lake Chad

2. Which two tributaries converge to form the Nile River in Khartoum, Sudan?

   a) White Nile and Niger River

   b) Blue Nile and Congo River

   c) White Nile and Blue Nile

   d) Blue Nile and Zambezi River

3. What ancient civilization is often referred to as the "gift of the Nile"?

   a) Mesopotamia

   b) Indus Valley Civilization

   c) Ancient Greece

   d) Ancient Egypt

4. What natural phenomenon contributed to the fertility of the soil along the Nile Delta in ancient Egypt?

   a) Volcanic eruptions

   b) Annual flooding

   c) Earthquakes

   d) Desertification

5. Which term describes the point at which two rivers meet and flow together?

a) Confluence

b) Tributary

c) Estuary

d) Delta

6. What term is used to describe species that are native to a specific region and found nowhere else?

a) Invasive

b) Indigenous

c) Endemic

d) Exotic

7. What do you call the countries or regions located along the banks of a river or other body of water?

a) Aquatic States

b) Coastal Nations

c) Riparian States

d) Hydro States

8. What is the ecological term for the variety of plant and animal life in a particular habitat or ecosystem?

a) Ecosystem Diversity

b) Habitat Variation

c) Biological Disparity

d) Faunal Spectrum

9. What is the approximate total length of the Nile River?

   a) 3,000 kilometers

   b) 4,500 miles

   c) 5,800 kilometers

   d) 6,650 kilometers

10. How has the geopolitical significance of the Nile River led to contemporary challenges among riparian states?

   a) Shared management strategies

   b) Disputes over water rights

   c) Joint ecological conservation efforts

   d) Cultural exchange programs

Answers

   1. b

   2. c

   3. d

   4. b

   5. a

   6. c

   7. c

   8. a

   9. d

   10. b

Nice Weather and Weekend Plans

Tim and Carrie are talking about their weekend plans.

Tim*:* The weather looks great for the weekend. Do you have any plans?

Carrie*:* I'm going to get my garden ready for planting. I have **my work cut out for me**. It's so overgrown. But, it's not **set in stone**. I'll see what else comes up!

Tim: Yeah, it is that time of year, right? The days are getting longer. I'm going to **play it by ear**. Honestly, I'm pretty **burned out** and am **barely treading water**. The **fallout** from the **cost-cutting measures** has had a huge impact on me.

Carrie*:* Sorry to hear that. Is there anything I can do to help?

Tim*:* Nah, it's okay. Gotta **bring home the bacon**, right? It's not all **doom and gloom**. I may go to a movie or something.

Carrie: You **got hit hard by** that. Don't you want to **throw in the towel?**

Vocabulary

my work cut out for me: A big or difficult job to do.

set in stone: Decided 100%.

burned out: Tired, stressed and overworked.

treading water: Barely keeping up with work or school.

fallout: Negative consequences.

cost-cutting measures: Something done to save money.

bring home the bacon: Make money with a job.

doom and gloom: Only bad things.

got hit hard by: To be badly affected by something.

throw in the towel: To quit or give up.

Practice

1. I'm barely _____ at my new job and am worried that I'll get fired.

2. We're not the only ones who _____ by Covid-19.

3. I hate my job but someone has to _____.

4. It's not all _____. He did get a B+ in English.

5. I have _____ with this new team.

6. I quit that job because I was so _____.

7. The _____ went too far I think. We're so understaffed now.

8. Nobody anticipated this would be the _____ from that decision.

9. Someone has to get fired but nothing is _____.

10. I'm ready to _____ on that project! It's brought me nothing but grief.

Answers

1. treading water

2. got hit hard by

3. bring home the bacon

4. doom and gloom

5. my work cut out for me

6. burned out

7. cost-cutting measures

8. fallout

9. set in stone

10. throw in the towel

Idioms #4

Damage control

Meaning: Trying to contain a bad situation; stop a bad thing from becoming worse.

Origin: Used literally since the 1950s to describe trying to contain damage on a ship. It's been used figuratively since the 1970s to describe any bad situation.

"Hasn't Keith already done *damage control* on this? Why are all these negative reviews still online?"

"We'll need to do *damage control*. The report was just leaked to the press."

Don't give up your day job

Meaning: A funny way to tell someone that you don't think they're good at something.

Origin: Uncertain.

(Did you like the dinner?) "Well Ted, *don't give up your day job!*"

(Have I gotten better at tennis since we played last?) "*Don't give up your day job.*"

Double down

Meaning: To double or increase a risk of a commitment because you are confident that it's going to succeed.

Origin: Refers to doubling your bet for a blackjack hand if you are confident that you're going to beat the dealer.

"Do you think we should *double down* on Pfizer stock? They're going to make a ton of money from their Covid-19 vaccine."

"I know you want to *double down* on real estate but I don't like to have all my money tied up in it."

Drive (someone) up the wall

Meaning: To annoy or frustrate a person to the point the person is extremely irritated or angry.

Origin: Possibly centuries old, but the origin is unclear. It could be referring to someone in prison trying to escape over the wall. Or, to a prisoner who is stopped at the wall.

"My son is *driving my husband up the wall*. I can't wait for summer vacation to be over."

"My employee *drives me up the wall* but he does great work so I don't think I can fire him."

Easy does it

Meaning: An expression used to tell someone to move slowly or carefully.

Origin: Possibly comes the Bible (Matthew 6:34) where it urges us to not worry about tomorrow.

"*Easy does it*. Don't go and play tennis for 3 hours. Your foot is finally better."

"Hey, *easy does it*, Tommy. Remember that last time you ate 6 pieces of pizza? You were so sick."

Eat your words

Meaning: To be forced to admit you were wrong about something.

Origin: Uncertain but traced back to the 1500s.

"You're going to have to *eat your words* and apologize to your dad I think."

"Don't worry too much about it. She'll eventually *eat her words* and take back what she said."

The Frightened Lion

Once upon a time in the heart of a vast **savanna**, there lived a powerful but frightened lion named Leo. Despite being the king of the jungle, Leo was afraid of many things. He feared the buzzing bees, the crackling thunderstorms, and even the tiny mice.

One day, Leo's animal friends gathered around him and noticed his anxious demeanor. A wise old elephant named Ella spoke up, "Leo, you are the **mightiest** lion in the jungle. Why do you let fear control you?"

Leo sighed and confessed, "I may be strong, but many things scare me. The buzzing of bees makes me nervous, the thunderstorms make me tremble, and even the smallest mice make me jump."

The animals decided to help Leo overcome his fears. They began with the buzzing bees. Slowly, Leo approached a beehive with the guidance of his friends. The bees, busy with their work, paid him no attention. Leo realized they were not interested in harming him.

Next, they faced the thunderstorms. The animals huddled together, and Leo learned that the thunder was just nature's way of making noise. The storm passed, and Leo felt a sense of relief.

Lastly, the mice. Leo's friends took him to meet a group of mice, and he saw they were more scared of him than he was of them. Leo realized that his fears were **unfounded**, and he felt a newfound confidence.

Leo thanked his friends for helping him **conquer** his fears. From that day on, he roared with strength, unburdened by unnecessary fears. The jungle celebrated the transformation of the once-frightened lion into a courageous and confident king.

The Moral

The moral of the story is that sometimes things that seem scary are not really as big as we think. With help from friends, we can be brave and face our fears.

Vocabulary

savannah: Grassland with few trees.

mightiest: The biggest.

unfounded: No foundation or basis in fact.

conquer: Overcome.

Comprehension Questions

1. What scared Leo the lion in the story?
2. Who noticed that Leo was always scared?
3. How did Leo's friends help him face his fear of bees?
4. What did Leo learn about thunderstorms with the help of his friends?
5. What made Leo feel braver in the end?

Answers

1. Leo was scared of buzzing bees, loud thunderstorms, and tiny mice.
2. Leo's friends, the other animals in the jungle, noticed that he was always scared.
3. They showed Leo that bees are busy and won't bother him if he doesn't bother them.
4. Leo learned that thunderstorms are just loud noises and not something to be afraid of.
5. Leo felt braver in the end because his friends showed him that the things he was scared of were not as big as he thought, and with their help, he could be strong and confident.

Online Dating

Jen and Tina are talking about online dating.

Jen: Hey, so what's new with you **these days**?

Tina: Oh, not much. But I did start doing **online dating**.

Jen: Nice! How's that going?

Tina: It's like finding a **needle in a haystack**. I mean, they don't have to look like **movie stars** but I'm so tired of guys with **facial hair**—**shaggy beards** and **bushy eyebrows**. Gross.

Jen: So what are you looking for?

Tina: Nothing complicated. Someone with an **athletic build**, **outgoing personality**, and a **good sense of humour**. Shouldn't be too difficult, right?

Vocabulary

these days: Lately; recently.

online dating: Finding a love match through the Internet.

needle in a haystack: Describes something that is difficult to find.

movie stars: Famous actors or actresses.

facial hair: Beard or mustache.

shaggy beards: Beards that are not well-groomed.

bushy eyebrows: Big eyebrows that are not well-groomed.

athletic build: Describes someone in good shape who exercises a lot.

outgoing personality: Describes someone who likes being around people.

good sense of humor: Describes someone who likes to laugh and tell jokes.

Practice

1. What have you been up to _____?

2. How did he get such an _____? He must be working out a lot.

3. Guys with _____ are all the rage lately.

4. Finding my keys in the morning is like finding a _____.

5. I love that my co-worker has such a _____. I'm always laughing.

6. Who are your favourite _____?

7. I'm thinking about growing out my _____. What do you think?

8. I hate my _____. It's so much work to keep them trimmed.

9. I'm looking for someone with an _____ because I'm kind of shy.

10. I know that you don't want to but I think you'd have good luck with _____.

Answers

1. these days

2. athletic build

3. shaggy beards

4. needle in a haystack

5. good sense of humour

6. movie stars

7. facial hair

8. bushy eyebrows

9. outgoing personality

10. online dating

Taking a Trip

Emma is talking to Alex about a vacation plan.

Alex: Hey, Emma! Long time no see! What have you been up to?

Emma: Hey, Alex! I've been thinking about taking a trip. I need to get away and unwind.

Alex: That's a fantastic idea! Where are you thinking of heading?

Emma: I'm thinking about **checking out** some tropical destinations. I've always wanted to **kick back** on a beach and **soak up** some sun.

Alex: Nice choice! Have you **narrowed down** your options, or are you still **looking up** different locations?

Emma: I've been browsing travel blogs and websites to get some ideas. I need to narrow it down and decide on the perfect spot.

Alex: If you need any help, feel free to reach out. I can **pitch in** with researching activities and places to visit.

Emma: Thanks, Alex! I might take you up on that offer. I also need to **sort through** my schedule and figure out the best time to **jet off**.

Alex: Absolutely! It's important to set aside some time for yourself. When do you plan to head out?

Emma: I'm thinking of **knocking out** work in the next few weeks and then taking off for a week or two.

Alex: Sounds like a plan! Once you've **nailed down** the details, let's meet up and go over your travel itinerary.

Emma: Great idea! I'll make sure to meet up with you before I take off. It'll be nice to catch up and get some travel tips.

Vocabulary

kick back: To relax or take it easy, often by reclining or lounging comfortably.

soak up: To enjoy or absorb completely, in this context, referring to enjoying the sun on a beach.

check out: To visit or explore a place, as mentioned in considering visiting tropical destinations.

narrow down: To reduce the number of options or choices, as in narrowing down travel destination choices.

look up: To search for information, as in looking up different locations on travel blogs and websites.

pitch in: To contribute or help, as mentioned in offering assistance with researching activities and places.

sort through: To organize or arrange by categorizing or selecting, in this context, referring to organizing one's schedule.

jet off: To depart or travel by airplane, as discussed in planning the departure for the trip.

knock out: To complete a task quickly and efficiently, as in knocking out work before the trip.

nail down: To finalize or determine, mentioned in finalizing the details of the travel plans.

Phrasal Verb Challenge

Fill in the blanks with the appropriate phrasal verbs:

1. After a hectic week at work, I can't wait to _____ and relax on the couch.

2. When on vacation, I love to _____ the local culture and traditions.

3. I need to _____ my schedule for the next month and figure out the best time to take a break.

4. Planning a trip can be overwhelming, but it helps to _____ the options and decide on a destination.

5. Before booking the flight, I always _____ information about the destination to ensure it's the right fit.

6. If you're unsure about your travel plans, feel free to ask for help, and I'll gladly _____ with the research.

7. To truly enjoy a new place, it's important to take some time to _____

the atmosphere and surroundings.

8. After a long day of exploring, it's nice to find a cozy spot to _____ and enjoy the sunset.

9. Once you've decided on the destination, make sure to _____ the necessary details, like accommodation and transportation.

10. To make the most of your trip, try to _____ work and other responsibilities before you leave.

Answers

1. kick back
2. soak up
3. sort through
4. narrow down
5. look up
6. pitch in
7. soak up
8. kick back
9. nail down
10. knock out

Comprehension Questions

1. Why does Emma want to take a trip?

2. What type of destinations is Emma considering for her trip?

3. How is Alex offering to help Emma with her travel plans?

4. How does Emma plan to decide on the perfect travel spot?

5. What does Emma do to get ideas for her trip?

6. How does Alex offer assistance in the planning process?

7. What does Emma need to sort through before planning her trip?

8. When does Emma plan to take off for her vacation?

9. What is the significance of the phrase "knocking out work" in the dialogue?

10. Why does Alex suggest meeting up before Emma takes off for her trip?

Answers

1. Emma wants to take a trip to get away and unwind.

2. Emma is considering tropical destinations.

3. Alex offers to help Emma by pitching in with researching activities and places.

4. Emma plans to decide on the perfect travel spot by narrowing down her options.

5. Emma gets ideas for her trip by browsing travel blogs and websites.

6. Alex offers assistance by suggesting they meet up to go over Emma's travel itinerary.

7. Emma needs to sort through her schedule before planning her trip.

8. Emma plans to take off for her vacation in the next few weeks.

9. "Knocking out work" refers to completing tasks quickly and efficiently before the trip.

10. Alex suggests meeting up before Emma takes off to catch up and provide travel tips.

You can't Judge a Book by Its Cover

Jerry and Linda are talking about one of their new neighbors.

Jerry: Have you met our new neighbor yet?

Linda: I talked to him last night but he's **a hard nut to crack**. He only gave one-word answers to all my questions!

Jerry: Well, **you can't judge a book by its cover**. I'm sure we'll find out more about him as time goes on. Maybe he's not that **talkative.**

Linda: Maybe. But I felt frustrated talking to him for just a few minutes. Anyway, I'm working on not **burning bridges** so I'll **put my best foot forward**!

Jerry: Good plan. You never know **what may come**. Let's invite him over for dinner and see if he **opens up**.

Vocabulary

you can't judge a book by its cover: to not judge something or someone based on appearance. For example, a restaurant that's not stylish and new may have delicious food.

a hard nut to crack: Someone that is difficult to get to know.

burning bridges: Damaging relationships.

put my best foot forward: To be on one's best behaviour.

what may come: What could happen in the future.

talkative: Someone who likes to talk a lot.

opens up: Shares information about oneself.

Practice

1. I try my best to avoid _____ when leaving a job.

2. I'm happy for the fresh start and want to _____ at this new job.

3. My dad rarely talks and is _____.

4. I learned early on in life that _____.

5. I'm well prepared for _____.

6. My daughter is so _____. I go for a walk every day to get a break!

7. I love it when my son _____ to me. It happens so rarely!

Answers

1. burning bridges

2. put my best foot forward

3. a hard nut to crack

4. you can't judge a book by its cover

5. what may come

6. talkative

7. opens up

Hand Preference

Hand preference, often colloquially referred to as "handedness," is a fascinating aspect of human behavior that reflects the dominance of one hand over the other in performing various tasks. While the majority of individuals exhibit a clear preference for either the right or left hand, the underlying mechanisms and the factors influencing hand preference remain subjects of ongoing scientific inquiry.

Biological Foundations

The roots of hand preference can be traced to the **intricate** interplay between genetics and brain lateralization. Studies have suggested a genetic component, indicating that the inclination to favor one hand over the other may be hereditary to some extent. Identical twins, who share nearly identical genetic material, are more likely to have similar hand preferences than non-identical twins or non-related individuals. However, the genetic influence is not **absolute**, as environmental factors also play a crucial role in shaping hand preference.

The brain's lateralization, where certain functions are localized to specific hemispheres, contributes significantly to hand preference. In most right-handed individuals, the left hemisphere of the brain controls language and motor functions, leading to the dominance of the right hand in various tasks. Conversely, left-handed individuals often exhibit a more balanced distribution of functions between the hemispheres or even a dominance of the right hemisphere.

Developmental Patterns

Hand preference begins to **manifest** during infancy, with infants as young as six months displaying a tendency to reach for objects with a preferred hand. As children grow, their hand preference becomes more pronounced, with many establishing a clear preference by the age of three or four. Interestingly, the transition from an initial lack of hand preference to the establishment of a dominant hand is a **dynamic** process influenced by environmental stimuli and neurological maturation.

Cultural and societal factors also contribute to the development of hand preference.

In many societies, right-handedness is the predominant **norm**, leading to a higher prevalence of right-handed individuals. This prevalence is not universal, and certain cultures exhibit a higher proportion of left-handed individuals. These variations highlight the complex interplay between biological predispositions and cultural influences.

Left-Handedness

Left-handed individuals, constituting roughly 10% of the population, have historically been subjects of intrigue and, at times, social stigma. Throughout history, left-handedness has been associated with superstitions and negative connotations. The term "sinister," derived from the Latin word for left, reflects the historical bias against left-handedness. However, societal attitudes have evolved, and contemporary perspectives recognize left-handedness as a natural and diverse aspect of human behavior.

The neurological basis for left-handedness is not fully understood, but it is believed to result from a combination of genetic and environmental factors. Some left-handed individuals may have a family history of left-handedness, suggesting a genetic predisposition. Environmental factors, such as exposure to certain hormones during fetal development, may also contribute to the development of left-handedness.

Ambidexterity

While most individuals exhibit a clear hand preference, some people display a degree of ambidexterity, the ability to use both hands with equal skill. True ambidexterity, where both hands are equally dominant, is relatively rare. In many cases, individuals may show ambidextrous tendencies for specific tasks while maintaining a clear overall hand preference. The development of ambidexterity is influenced by both genetic factors and deliberate practice in using both hands.

Conclusion

In conclusion, hand preference is a multifaceted phenomenon shaped by genetic, neurological, developmental, and cultural factors. While the majority of individuals exhibit a clear preference for one hand, the diversity of hand preferences, including left-handedness and ambidexterity, adds a rich layer to the complexity of human behavior. As our understanding of the brain and genetics continues to advance, the exploration of hand preference offers insights into the intricacies of human development and the interplay between nature and nurture in shaping individual characteristics.

Vocabulary

lateralization: The specialization of functions in the left or right hemisphere of the brain.

genetics: The study of heredity and the variation of inherited characteristics.

ambidexterity: The ability to use both hands with equal skill.

hereditary: Passing of genetic traits or characteristics from parent to offspring.

superstitions: Beliefs or practices resulting from irrational fear of the unknown or unexplainable.

neurological: Pertaining to the nervous system, especially the brain and nerves.

predisposition: A tendency or inclination toward a particular condition or behavior.

norm: A standard or pattern that is considered typical or usual within a society or group.

stigma: A mark of disgrace or shame associated with a particular quality or characteristic.

intricate: Complicated, detailed, and complex in structure or design.

Vocabulary Challenge

1. Intricate, in the second paragraph is closest in meaning to:

   a) complicated

   b) confusing

   c) having many, interrelated parts

   d) too detailed to understand

2. Absolute, in the second paragraph is closest in meaning to:

   a) the only thing

   b) a moral principle

   c) inflexible

   d) a brand of Vodka

3. Manifest, in the fourth paragraph is most closely related to:

   a) a political idea

   b) obvious

   c) the appearance of a ghost or spirit

   d) show

4. Dynamic, in the fourth paragraph is most closely related to:

   a) a positive attitude

   b) changing

   c) related to electronics

   d) related to the volume of sound produced

5. Norm, in the fifth paragraph is most closely related to:

   a) short for "normal"

   b) typical or standard

   c) something that must always be done

   d) a mathematical term

Answers

1. c

2. a

3. d

4. b

5. b

Comprehension Questions

1. What is lateralization in the context of hand preference?

   a) The dominance of one hand over the other

   b) The ability to use both hands equally

   c) The specialization of functions in the brain hemispheres

   d) The influence of cultural factors on hand use

2. Which term refers to the passing of genetic traits from parent to offspring?

   a) Ambidexterity

   b) Lateralization

   c) Hereditary

   d) Predisposition

3. What does the term "ambidexterity" describe?

   a) The dominance of one hand over the other

   b) The ability to use both hands equally

   c) The preference for using the left hand

   d) The inclination to use the right hand

4. What does the term "hereditary" mean in the context of hand preference?

   a) Passing of genetic traits

   b) Cultural influence on hand use

   c) Environmental factors affecting hand preference

   d) Personal choice of hand use

5. In the historical context, what negative association has been linked to left-handedness?

   a) Strength and power

   b) Superior intelligence

   c) Sinister connotations

   d) Cultural admiration

6. What does the term "neurological" pertain to in the discussion of hand preference?

   a) Genetic traits

   b) Brain and nerves

   c) Cultural norms

   d) Environmental influences

7. What is a "predisposition" in the context of hand preference?

   a) The ability to use both hands equally

   b) A tendency or inclination toward a particular behavior

   c) Passing of genetic traits

   d) A historical negative association

8. What is a "norm" regarding hand preference?

   a) A tendency or inclination toward a particular behavior

   b) A standard or pattern considered typical within a society

   c) The passing of genetic traits

   d) The ability to use both hands equally

131

9. What does the term "stigma" mean in the context of hand preference?

   a) A tendency or inclination toward a particular behavior

   b) Passing of genetic traits

   c) A mark of disgrace or shame associated with a characteristic

   d) The ability to use both hands equally

10. What does the term "intricate" mean in the discussion of hand preference?

   a) The passing of genetic traits

   b) Complicated, detailed, and complex in structure or design

   c) The ability to use both hands equally

   d) A standard or pattern considered typical within a society

Answers

   1. c

   2. c

   3. b

   4. a

   5. c

   6. b

   7. b

   8. b

   9. c

   10. b

A Dilemma

Kevin and Tracy are talking about a situation at work.

Tracy: How are things going with your team?

Kevin: Not great. We keep missing deadlines and getting work sent back because it's not high enough quality. I don't know how to **mend** things. It's a real **dilemma**. As their **intrepid** leader, I feel like I've failed. I've tried to **evaluate** what's going on, but I'm not sure.

Tracy: Well, team **cohesion** is key. The **fundamental flaw** of your team seems to be a lack of team spirit. You need to be **cognizant** of the relationships between people.

Kevin: I'm terrible at that. That must be why we're struggling.

Tracy: Focus on creating a positive atmosphere. **Praise** goes a long way too!

Kevin: I'm happy that I talked to you about this.

Vocabulary

mend: To fix.

dilemma: A Situation requiring a difficult choice.

intrepid: Fearless.

evaluate: Assess.

cohesion: Uniting, or becoming one.

fundamental: Basic; of primary importance.

flaw: A feature that ruins the perfection of something.

cognizant: Being aware of something.

praise: To give approval or admiration.

Practice

1. Do you think we can _____ that zipper instead of throwing it out?

2. _____ is key to any team.

3. I have a _____. I said that I'd be in two places at the same time!

4. Please be _____ of that fact that I'm terribly out of shape! You'll have to walk a bit slower.

5. The _____ problem is that we have a hard time talking to each other.

6. Let's _____ what went wrong here.

7. A bit of _____ goes a long way! Tell people when they do a good job of something.

8. You're such an _____ traveler! I can't believe you did that by yourself.

9. It looks great. The only _____ is that you didn't cite your references in the correct format.

Answers

1. mend

2. cohesion

3. dilemma

4. cognizant

5. fundamental

6. evaluate

7. praise

8. intrepid

9. flaw

134

The Dog and His Reflection

In a small village, there lived a friendly dog named Max. Max was known for his shiny coat and **wagging** tail. One day, as Max was strolling near a sparkling pond, he noticed something peculiar - another dog just like him! Max barked at the other dog, and it barked back. He wagged his tail, and the other dog did the same.

Deciding to investigate further, Max jumped into the **pond**, creating ripples in the water. To his surprise, the other dog did the same. Max spun around in excitement, and again, the dog in the water copied his every move.

Max thought he had found the most wonderful playmate. He **barked** louder, wagged his tail faster, and even did a little dance. Each time, the dog in the water mimicked him perfectly.

Feeling proud of his new friend, Max continued his antics until he noticed something strange. When he dropped a stick into the water, the other dog didn't drop one back. Instead, the stick disappeared into the depths of the pond. Confused, Max realized that the other dog wasn't a real friend but just his own **reflection** in the water. He felt a bit silly but also learned an important lesson.

From that day on, whenever Max saw his reflection, he remembered not to be fooled by appearances. He knew that real friends were the ones who shared sticks and played together in the sunshine.

The Moral

The moral of the story is to be careful not to be fooled by appearances. It's important to distinguish between what's real and what's just a reflection. True friends are the ones who share and play together, not just those who mimic our actions.

Vocabulary

pond: A small body of water (smaller than a lake).

wagging: Moving a tail of an animal around quickly.

reflection: An image seen on a shiny surface like water or a mirror.

barked: Made a sound (dog).

Comprehension Questions

1. What did Max notice near the pond one sunny day?

2. Why did Max think he found a new friend?

3. What did Max realize when he dropped a stick into the water?

4. What lesson did Max learn from the experience?

5. How did Max feel when he discovered the truth about the water dog?

Answers

1. Max noticed another dog that looked just like him, but in the water.

2. Max thought he found a new friend because the other dog in the water mimicked his actions and played with him.

3. Max realized that the other dog in the water wasn't a real friend because it didn't give the stick back.

4. Max learned not to be fooled by appearances and to look for real friends who share and play together.

5. Max felt a bit silly when he realized the water dog was just his reflection, not a real friend.

Complaining about a Co-worker

Jerry is telling Linda about a fight he had with a coworker.

Jerry: I just had a big fight with my friend and I'm not sure I can just **get over it.** It was a **massive blow-up**.

Linda*:* Oh no! What happened?

Jerry*:* Well, she's my co-worker and keeps **stealing my thunder** on work projects. She's taking credit for stuff that I do. I'm **sick and tired of it.** I just caught her **red-handed**.

Linda: That's a **tough pill to swallow**. I'd for sure have a **bee in my bonnet** about this too.

Jerry*:* It's not even **the straw that broke the camel's back.** She owes me a thousand **bucks** as well.

Linda*:* Honestly, she sounds like a **bad egg**.

Vocabulary

stealing my thunder: Taking credit for something that someone else did.

get over it: To fully recover (from an illness) or not think about it negatively anymore (break-up with a girlfriend or boyfriend, losing a job, etc.).

tough pill to swallow: Something difficult to get over.

bee in my bonnet: A certain issue that is annoying someone.

the straw that broke the camel's back: The last thing in a series of bad things before an event occurs — like a breakup, quitting a job, or fight.

blow-up: Big fight or problem.

massive: Very big/huge.

sick and tired of it: Annoyed by something that happens frequently.

bucks: Dollars.

red-handed: Caught doing something bad.

bad egg: A bad or dishonest person.

Practice

1. He looks like a million _____ these days.

2. I get a _____ any time I deal with that certain customer at work.

3. My mom is pretty relaxed but she would have a big _____ every once in a while.

4. Tony got fired after his boss caught him stealing _____.

5. He got a _____ raise at work. Lucky guy!

6. My teammate keeps _____ and always seems to forget that I set him up for most of his goals.

7. Getting a D on that test was a _____.

8. I can't just _____. I'm still in love with my ex-boyfriend.

9. That last project was _____ before I quit.

10. My mom is _____. She's gone on strike!

11. One _____ can negatively influence an entire company.

Answers

1. bucks

2. bee in my bonnet

3. blow-up

4. red-handed

5. massive

6. stealing my thunder

7. tough pill to swallow

8. get over it

9. the straw that broke the camel's back

10. sick and tired of it

11. bad egg

The Daily Grind

Sarah is talking about how she completes her daily tasks.

Chris: Hey, Sarah! Long time no see! How's everything going?

Sarah: Hi, Chris! All good, just caught up in my daily grind. You know how it is.

Chris: Totally get that. What does a typical day look like for you?

Sarah: Well, I usually wake up early and **kick off** my day by checking emails. Then, I try to **sort through** the priorities for the day.

Chris: Nice! How do you manage to **chip away at** your tasks?

Sarah: I **break down** my to-do list and tackle each task one by one. It helps me stay on top of things without feeling overwhelmed.

Chris: Impressive! Do you have any specific activities you like to mix in during the day?

Sarah: Absolutely! I always set aside some time to **catch up on** industry news. It's essential to **look up** trends and stay informed.

Chris: True. I also heard you've been thinking about taking up a workout routine.

Sarah: Yes, I've been trying to incorporate exercise into my daily routine. I need to take care of my well-being.

Chris: That's a fantastic initiative! How do you plan to fit it into your busy schedule?

Sarah: I'm thinking of **carving out** time in the evenings. I'll need to figure out the best way to balance work and personal goals.

Chris: Good call. It's crucial to set aside time for yourself. When do you plan to start?

Sarah: I'm hoping to start next week. I just need to **nail down** the details and find a workout routine that works for me.

Vocabulary

catch up on: To become involved in something, often a routine or work tasks.

kick off: To start or initiate, usually referring to the beginning of an activity or day.

sort through: To organize or examine items or information systematically, often to prioritize or make sense of them.

chip away at: To make gradual progress by working persistently on a task, bit by bit.

break down: To divide a complex task or list into smaller, more manageable parts for easier execution.

look up: To search for information or references, often online, as mentioned in staying informed about industry trends.

catch up on: To bring oneself up to date, typically by completing tasks that were neglected or by staying informed.

carve out: To create or designate time for a specific purpose within a busy schedule.

nail down: To finalize or determine the details of a plan or decision, as discussed in planning a workout routine.

Phrasal Verb Challenge

Fill in the blanks with the appropriate phrasal verbs:

1. After a long vacation, Sarah needed to _____ her work tasks and emails.

2. Let's _____ the new project with a team meeting this Friday.

3. I have a messy desk, and I need to _____ the documents and prioritize the urgent ones.

4. Instead of feeling overwhelmed, it's better to _____ the project into smaller tasks.

5. Don't forget to _____ the latest industry trends before our meeting tomorrow.

6. It's essential to _____ time for self-care, even in the midst of a busy schedule.

7. I've been trying to _____ a healthier lifestyle by incorporating exercise into my routine.

8. Before we proceed, let's _____ the details of the upcoming event and finalize our plans.

Answers

1. catch up on
2. kick off
3. sort through
4. chip away at
5. look up
6. carve out
7. chip away at
8. nail down

Comprehension Questions

1. Why does Sarah want to take up a workout routine?
2. How does Chris offer to help Sarah with her workout routine?
3. What part of the day does Sarah plan to allocate for exercise?
4. What does Sarah mean by "nailing down the details" of her workout routine?
5. How does Sarah typically start her day?
6. According to Sarah, why is it important to break down tasks on her to-do list?
7. What role does looking up information play in Sarah's daily routine?
8. Why does Chris suggest carving out time for self-care?
9. How does Sarah suggest she will balance work and personal goals?

Answers

1. Sarah wants to take up a workout routine to kick back and take care of her well-being.

2. Chris offers to help Sarah by letting her know he's available for support and assistance.

3. Sarah plans to carve out time in the evenings for exercise.

4. "Nailing down the details" means finalizing or determining the specific aspects of Sarah's workout routine.

5. Sarah typically starts her day by waking up early and checking emails.

6. Sarah believes breaking down tasks on her to-do list helps her stay on top of things without feeling overwhelmed.

7. Looking up information is crucial for Sarah to stay informed about industry trends.

8. Chris suggests carving out time for self-care to ensure Sarah takes a break and relaxes.

9. Sarah plans to balance work and personal goals by figuring out the best way to integrate exercise into her schedule.

The Last Straw

Jerry is talking to Linda about wanting to leave his wife.

Jerry: So I think I'm going to **leave my wife**.

Linda: On no! What happened? You guys always seemed like pretty **happy campers** to me.

Jerry: Well, **the last straw** was looking at my retirement accounts and seeing that most of them were **cleaned out**. Plus, we're in the red on all our other accounts too. She loves to **shop till she drops** but I didn't realize how **dire** it was until now.

Linda: Sorry to hear that. I hope you can get back **in the black**. You went **from rags to riches** once. I'm sure you can do it again.

Jerry: Hopefully, but after paying the divorce lawyers, I'll have a lot of work to **make up for lost time** on those retirement accounts. And she may also want **spousal support**.

Linda: Well, hang in there my friend. I'm here for you.

Vocabulary

the last straw: The final annoying thing before someone loses their patience. For example, a child has been misbehaving all day but his dad finally yelled at him when he wouldn't stay in his room at bedtime.

in the black: To not be in debt.

leave my wife: Separate or get a divorce.

happy campers: People that are joyful or having fun together.

cleaned out: Usually refers to money, when someone spends everything.

shop till she drops: Loves shopping and spends lots of time doing it.

dire: Very bad.

make up for lost time: Wasted time that you can't get back.

spousal support: Money paid to a former husband or wife after getting divorced.

from rags to riches: Poor to rich.

Practice

1. The food situation is now becoming _____. One of us has to go shopping!

2. Honestly, this is _____ before he gets fired.

3. We started living frugally and are now _____.

4. I want to _____. We just don't have that much in common anymore.

5. The kids were such _____ when I bought them a new trampoline.

6. My wife loves to _____ but I feel nervous about how much money she's spending.

7. I had to pay _____ after getting divorced.

8. I only started dating in my twenties. Now, I have to _____.

9. Wow! I love the story of that guy going _____ when he moved to the USA.

Answers

1. dire

2. the last straw

3. in the black

4. leave my wife

5. happy campers

6. shop till she drops

7. spousal support

8. make up for lost time

9. from rags to riches

The Enigma of Dinosaur Extinction

The extinction of dinosaurs, marking the end of the Mesozoic Era about 66 million years ago, stands as a **captivating** and transformative event in Earth's history. Unraveling the mysteries surrounding this mass extinction involves exploring the interplay of cosmic and terrestrial factors that forever **altered** the planet's ecosystems.

Asteroid Impact Hypothesis: Unveiling Catastrophe

At the **heart** of the extinction **narrative** lies the asteroid impact hypothesis, suggesting a colossal asteroid struck near the Yucatan Peninsula, creating the Chicxulub crater and triggering a chain of catastrophic events. The immediate aftermath included wildfires, earthquakes, and a mega-tsunami. The ensuing "impact winter," caused by debris in the atmosphere, led to a dramatic reduction in sunlight, severely disrupting ecosystems by **hampering** photosynthesis.

Volcanic Activity: The Earth's Fury Unleashed

In tandem with the asteroid impact, extensive volcanic activity in the Deccan Traps of India added to the environmental turmoil. The eruption of lava released significant amounts of greenhouse gases, including carbon dioxide and sulfur dioxide, potentially contributing to climate change, altered weather patterns, and further stressing ecosystems already reeling from the asteroid impact.

Consequences on Life: The Demise and the Rise

The combined environmental upheaval resulted in profound consequences for life on Earth. Iconic species like Tyrannosaurus rex and Triceratops faced extinction, along with marine reptiles, ammonites, and various plant species. Simultaneously, the extinction event provided opportunities for mammals, previously overshadowed by dinosaurs, to flourish. The rise of mammals into diverse ecological roles eventually set the stage for the emergence of modern mammals, including humans.

Confirmation through Geological Clues

The asteroid impact hypothesis finds crucial support in geological evidence. The discovery of an iridium-rich sediment layer, shocked quartz, and microtektites in the geologic record aligns with the aftermath of an extraterrestrial impact. Additionally, geological studies of the Deccan Traps lava flows help establish the timing of volcanic activity in relation to the mass extinction event.

Ongoing Exploration: Refining the Extinction Story

While the asteroid impact hypothesis is widely accepted, ongoing research continues to refine our understanding of the specific sequence of events and the relative importance of each contributing factor. Advances in geology, paleontology, and astrobiology contribute to a more comprehensive narrative of this pivotal moment in Earth's history.

Conclusion

In conclusion, the extinction of dinosaurs remains a captivating tale, woven with cosmic collisions, volcanic fury, and the resilience of life. The legacy of this mass extinction event endures in the fossil record, offering valuable insights into the interconnected web of Earth's history and the ever-evolving drama of life on our planet.

Vocabulary

extinction: The complete disappearance of a species or group of organisms from Earth.

Mesozoic era: The geological era that spans from approximately 252 to 66 million years ago, characterized by the dominance of dinosaurs and the evolution of various plant and animal groups.

cataclysmic: Involving or causing a sudden and violent upheaval, often with widespread and severe consequences.

interplay: The dynamic interaction or reciprocal influence of different elements.

photosynthesis: The process by which green plants and some other organisms convert light energy into chemical energy, producing oxygen and carbohydrates from carbon dioxide and water.

Iridium: A dense, corrosion-resistant metal that is rare on Earth's surface but often associated with extraterrestrial objects such as asteroids.

tsunami: A series of ocean waves with extremely long wavelengths and high energy, typically caused by underwater disturbances such as earthquakes or asteroid impacts.

greenhouse gases: Gases in the Earth's atmosphere, such as carbon dioxide and methane, that trap heat and contribute to the greenhouse effect, leading to an increase in global temperatures.

ecological niches: The role or function of an organism or species within an ecosystem, including how it obtains and utilizes resources and interacts with other organisms.

Paleontology: The scientific study of the history of life on Earth through the examination of plant and animal fossils.

Vocabulary Challenge
1. Captivating, in the first paragraph is closest in meaning to:
   a) attracting and holding interest
   b) key
   c) unknown
   d) holding hostage

2. Altered, in the first paragraph is closest in meaning to:

   a) tailored

   b) made structural changes to a building

   c) had a small impact

   d) changed

3. Heart, in the second paragraph is closest in meaning to:

   a) a body part

   b) a shape

   c) part of something

   d) the central part of something

4. Narrative, in the second paragraph is most closely related to:

   a) distinct from dialogue

   b) story

   c) a kind of poem

   d) part of a movie

5. Hampering, in the second paragraph is most closely related to:

   a) slowing down

   b) going at the same speed

   c) stopping completely

   d) speeding up

Answers

   1. a

   2. d

   3. d

   4. b

   5. a

Comprehension Questions

1. What is the Mesozoic Era known for?

   a) Ice ages

   b) Dominance of dinosaurs

   c) Rise of mammals

   d) Human civilization

2. What process involves converting light energy into chemical energy, producing oxygen and carbohydrates?

   a) Respiration

   b) Photosynthesis

   c) Decomposition

   d) Fermentation

3. What metal is often associated with extraterrestrial objects such as asteroids and is crucial evidence supporting the asteroid impact hypothesis?

   a) Iron

   b) Iridium

   c) Gold

   d) Copper

4. Which geological era spans from approximately 252 to 66 million years ago and is characterized by the dominance of dinosaurs?

   a) Paleozoic Era

   b) Cenozoic Era

   c) Mesozoic Era

   d) Precambrian Era

5. What term describes the interaction or reciprocal influence of different elements, such as factors contributing to the extinction of dinosaurs?

a) Cataclysmic

b) Mesozoic

c) Interplay

d) Extinction

6. Which natural disaster, often triggered by underwater disturbances, involves a series of ocean waves with long wavelengths and high energy?

a) Hurricane

b) Earthquake

c) Tsunami

d) Tornado

7. What is the process by which organisms break down organic matter, returning essential nutrients to the ecosystem?

a) Photosynthesis

b) Decomposition

c) Fermentation

d) Respiration

8. What gases, including carbon dioxide and methane, contribute to the greenhouse effect and global warming?

a) Nitrogen and oxygen

b) Hydrogen and helium

c) Greenhouse gases

d) Sulfur dioxide and nitrogen oxides

9. What term describes the complete disappearance of a species or group of organisms from Earth?

   a) Evolution

   b) Extinction

   c) Adaptation

   d) Speciation

10. What scientific field focuses on the study of the history of life on Earth through the examination of plant and animal fossils?

   a) Geology

   b) Biology

   c) Paleontology

   d) Archaeology

Answers

   1. b

   2. b

   3. b

   4. c

   5. c

   6. c

   7. b

   8. c

   9. b

   10. c

Highly Effective

Jim and John are talking about managing money.

Jim: Hey John. I'm wondering how you and Tina manage your money? It's a **key issue** for Jen and I and we need to come up with a better system.

John: We've been **married for 20 years** now and have a **joint account**. What works for us is that we're **brutally honest** about what we spend our money on. We don't **keep secrets**.

Jim: You're married to a keeper. That's for sure. Jen is **between jobs** and I'm **worried sick** about it. We may have to **borrow money** from the bank to **pay the mortgage**.

John: Sorry to hear that. When **money was tight** for us, we found a **highly effective** budgeting system. It could work for you.

Vocabulary

key issue: The most important thing.

married for _____ years: Number of years after a wedding that two people are together.

joint account: A bank account that two or more people hold together.

brutally honest: Holding nothing back from each other; no secrets.

keep secrets: Not telling important information.

between jobs: Describes someone who lost a job but is looking for another one.

worried sick: Anxious or stressed out to the extreme.

borrow money: Get a loan.

money was tight: Not enough money.

highly effective: Describes something that works very well.

Practice

1. Tony and I have been _____.

2. Can I be _____ with you? This partnership just isn't working out for us.

3. I don't want to _____ from each other anymore. It makes our relationship difficult.

4. Tim always seems to be _____. I wonder what's up with him?

5. _____ when I was going to medical school.

6. I know that you're _____ about it but get some sleep.

7. I've heard that it's a _____ system for losing weight.

8. Why don't we open up a _____? It would make things easier.

9. Let's try to _____ to make it through these next few weeks.

Answers

1. married for 10 years

2. brutally honest

3. keep secrets

4. between jobs

5. money was tight

6. worried sick

7. highly effective

8. joint account

9. borrow money

Idioms #5

Hang in there

Meaning: A way to tell someone not to give up because circumstances will improve.

Origin: 2 possible origins:

1. From competitive sport in the USA in the 1950s. Used as an encouragement to teammates.

2. From a motivational poster in the 1960s/70s that said "Hang in there, baby!"

"*Hang in there.* I know it's difficult but your final exam is just around the corner."

"*Hang in there*, okay? I know breakups are always difficult but it will get better with time."

Hard to swallow

Meaning: Something that is difficult to believe or accept.

Origin: From the 17th century. It refers to pills that are sometimes hard to swallow. It originated as bitter (a bitter pill to swallow) and evolved to hard later on. It can be heard as "tough to swallow," or, "A tough pill to swallow."

"Honestly, his excuse is *hard to swallow.* I just don't believe that he was sick the day before a long weekend."

"Getting fired was *hard to swallow*, especially after I put my heart and soul into that company."

Has the cat got your tongue?

Meaning: Used to get someone to talk when they're being unusually quiet.

Origin: Uncertain.

"**The cat got your tongue**? Say hi to your cousins."

"Has *the cat got your tongue*? You have to say hi to people when they say hi to you."

154

Have a blast

Meaning: "Have fun" at some event, party, etc.

Origin: It could be related to the blast furnace from the 1700s where air was forced into a furnace to facilitate combustion for iron smelting. It was very noisy.

"I'm *having a blast*! Let's stay for a bit longer."

"*Have a blast* at your party tonight!"

Have a crush on (someone)

Meaning: The initial stages of a romantic attraction to someone.

Origin: Traced to the 1884 journal of Isabella Maud Rittenhouse about a romantic interest.

"I *have a crush on* my new co-worker. She's not only cute but funny too!"

"Did you hear that Ted *has a crush on* Tina? Do you think he's going to ask her out?"

In the blink of an eye

Other forms: In the twinkling of an eye (earlier version). It's used less commonly now.

Meaning: In an instant.

Origin: The earlier version (in the twinkling of an eye) is seen as early as the Bible (1 Corinthians 15:51-52).

"It all happened *in the blink of an eye*. One day I was young and carefree and now my kids are all grown up."

"My life changed *in the blink of an eye* when I got into that accident."

It's the best thing since sliced bread

Meaning: Something or someone that is useful or good, Refers to the best thing that has come around in a long time.

Origin: Most likely refers to a Wonderbread advertising Slogan (the first company to manufacture pre-sliced, pre-wrapped bread).

"This new TV series is *the best thing since sliced bread*! I love it so much."

"That new guy? He's *the best thing since sliced bread*, right?"

Jump ship

Meaning: To leave or quit something abruptly, because you thought it was failing.

Origin: Refers to a sailor wishing to leave the ship without permission—thus jumping off the ship.

"Your company is about to go bankrupt. Don't you think it's time to *jump ship*?"

"If you want to *jump ship*, that's fine but I think you're probably making a big mistake. Your company is struggling now but I think they're going to recover quickly."

Jump through hoops

Meaning: To do a series of complicated or unnecessary series of things to accomplish or achieve something.

Origin: Refers to circus tricks and animals that are forced by handlers to jump through hoops (at times on fire). This is often done through force by the use of whips.

"If you want to teach English in South Korea, you have to *jump through hoops* with all the paperwork."

"The worst thing about starting a new job is having to *jump through hoops* during the application and onboarding processes."

156

A Bundle of Sticks

Once upon a time in a small village, there lived a family of five **siblings**. They were always **arguing** and fighting, and their parents worried about the constant discord. To teach them a valuable lesson, their wise grandmother decided to share the fable of the **Bundle** of Sticks.

One day, Grandma gathered the siblings and handed each of them a single stick. She asked them to break it, and each sibling easily snapped their stick in two. Next, Grandma handed each sibling a bundle of five sticks tied together. She challenged them to break the bundle. No matter how hard they tried, none of the siblings could break the bundle of sticks.

Grandma smiled and said, "You see, my dear ones, individually, you are like those single sticks—fragile and easily broken. But together, as a united bundle, you are strong and unbreakable." The siblings looked at each other, realizing the wisdom in Grandma's words. From that day on, they decided to stick together, supporting and helping each other through thick and thin.

The village noticed the positive change in the siblings, and their **newfound** unity brought peace and happiness to their home. The lesson of the Bundle of Sticks stayed with them throughout their lives, reminding them that strength comes from unity and cooperation. And so, the once-fighting siblings learned the power of togetherness, creating a strong **bond** that lasted a lifetime.

The moral of the story is that **unity** is strength. Just like a bundle of sticks is harder to break than a single stick, people working together can overcome challenges more easily.

The Moral

The moral of the story is that when people work together and support each other, they become stronger. Like a bunch of sticks tied together is harder to break than a single stick, unity and cooperation help us face challenges and difficulties in life.

Vocabulary

siblings: 2 or more children sharing a mother and/or father.

bundle: A collection of things wrapped together.

arguing: Expressing opinions in an angry way.

newfound: Recently discovered.

unity: The state of being joined, or of having the same opinion.

bond: A relationship between people or grounds.

Comprehension Questions

1. What was the problem with the five brothers and sisters in the story?
2. What did Grandma give each sibling to break?
3. Could the siblings easily break the single sticks?
4. What did Grandma give them next, and could they break it?
5. What did the siblings learn from this experience?

Answers

1. They always fought with each other.
2. Grandma gave each sibling a single stick.
3. Yes, they could easily break the single sticks.
4. Grandma gave them a bundle of sticks tied together, and they couldn't break it.
5. They learned that when they stay together and support each other, they are stronger, just like a bundle of sticks is harder to break than a single stick.

Hit the Books

Jerry is talking to Linda about having to study for an exam.

Jerry: I've been **breaking out in a cold sweat** a lot lately. I'm not used to having to **hit the books**.

Linda: What are you studying for?

Jerry: I have to pass this exam for work and I'll lose my job if I don't. I'm maybe **making a mountain of a molehill** but I can't help being nervous about it. It's been so long since I've had to take a test.

Linda: It's **like riding a bike**. You'll get back into it once you start. **Go with the flow**.

Jerry: Do you have any **study tips**?

Linda: My best advice is to study a little bit every day instead of **pulling all-nighters** or **cramming**. That doesn't work.

Vocabulary

breaking out in a cold sweat: To be afraid or nervous about something.

hit the books: When someone spends time studying.

go with the flow: To relax and go along with whatever.

making a mountain out of a molehill: To make something into a bigger deal than it is. For example, someone who loses sleep over a small problem.

like riding a bike: Something that you always remember how to do, even with a large break in between.

study tips: Ideas for how to study more effectively.

pulling all-nighters: Staying up all night to study or work.

cramming: Trying to learn everything for a test at the last minute.

Practice

1. Dude, sorry I can't hang out. I need to _____.

2. You'll get the hang of it. It's _____.

3. Before the second date, I kept _____. That's a bad sign, right?

4. I think you need to _____ with this school project. It sounds like you're taking it way more seriously than the other people in your group.

5. I don't think that _____ is a very effective study method.

6. One of the best _____ is to do it for one hour and then take a 10-minute break.

7. My days of _____ are over. I'm too old for that!

8. I think you're _____. It's not a big deal!

Answers

1. hit the books

2. like riding a bike

3. breaking out in a cold sweat

4. go with the flow

5. cramming

6. study tips

7. pulling all-nighters

8. making a mountain out of a molehill

At a Restaurant

A customer is ordering something at a restaurant.

Waiter: Good evening! Have you had a chance to look over the menu, or would you like a few more minutes?

Customer: Hi! We've already checked it out. We're ready to **place an order.**

Waiter: Great! What can I get you for starters?

Customer: We'd like to **start off** with the spinach and artichoke dip, please.

Waiter: Excellent choice! And for the main course?

Customer: I think I'll **go for** the grilled salmon, and she's planning to **opt for** the vegetable stir-fry.

Waiter: Perfect! How would you like your salmon cooked?

Customer: I'll have it **cooked through**, please.

Waiter: Noted. And any specific preferences for the stir-fry?

Customer: She'd like it with extra tofu, and can you **leave out** the mushrooms?

Waiter: Of course! And to drink?

Customer: We'll **go with** a bottle of the house red wine.

Waiter: Fantastic! I'll get that **sorted out** for you. Anything else?

Customer: Actually, we're **up for** some dessert later. Could you recommend something sweet?

Waiter: Absolutely! I'd suggest trying our chocolate lava cake. It's a hit among our customers.

Customer: Sounds delicious! We'll definitely **save room for** dessert. Thanks!

Waiter: My pleasure! I'll **check back** with you once your main courses are finished. Enjoy your meal!

Vocabulary

place an order: To request and specify items from a menu in a restaurant or while shopping.

start off: To begin a meal or event with a particular dish or activity.

go for: To choose or select, often from available options.

opt for: To choose or prefer one option over others.

cook through: To cook something completely, ensuring it is thoroughly done.

leave out: To exclude or not include a particular ingredient or item.

go with: To choose or select a particular option, often used for preferences or decisions.

sorted out: To handle or manage a situation, often involving organization or resolution.

up for: Willing or ready to participate in or enjoy something.

save room for: To intentionally leave space or capacity for something, typically used in the context of saving space for dessert.

check back: To return or revisit, often used in the context of reviewing progress or attending to needs.

Phrasal Verb Challenge

Fill in the blanks with the appropriate phrasal verbs:

1. The waiter approached the table and asked if they were ready to

   _____.

2. We decided to _____ our meal with a light salad.

3. After perusing the menu, Sarah chose to _____ the grilled chicken for dinner.

4. The chef recommended the pasta dish, but I think I'll _____ the seafood risotto instead.

5. I prefer my steak to be _____, so please make sure it's thoroughly cooked.

6. When ordering the pizza, I'd like them to _____ the olives; I'm not a fan of them.

7. For drinks, we'll _____ a bottle of the house white wine.

8. The waiter assured us that he would have our special requests

   _____.

9. The chocolate lava cake on the dessert menu sounded tempting, so we decided we

   were _____ it.

10. Even though we were full, we managed to _____ dessert because it

    sounded too delicious to pass up.

11. The waiter promised to _____ with us after serving the main courses

    to see if everything was satisfactory.

Answers

1. place an order
2. start off
3. opt for
4. go for
5. cooked through
6. leave out
7. go with
8. sorted out
9. up for
10. save room for
11. check back

Comprehension Questions

1. How does the waiter begin the interaction with the customers?

2. What appetizer do the customers choose to start their meal?

3. What does the customer decide to order for the main course?

4. How does the customer express their preference for the seafood risotto?

5. How does the customer want their steak to be prepared?

6. What special request does the customer make for the pizza order?

7. What drink do the customers select to accompany their meal?

8. What assurance does the waiter give regarding the special requests?

9. What dessert option do the customers express interest in trying?

10. Why do the customers decide to save room for dessert, even though they were already full?

Answers

1. The waiter begins the interaction by asking if the customers are ready to place an order.

2. The customers choose to start off their meal with a spinach and artichoke dip.

3. The customer decides to go for the grilled salmon for the main course.

4. The customer expresses their preference for the seafood risotto by saying they'll opt for it.

5. The customer wants their steak to be cooked through.

6. The customer makes a special request to leave out the olives on the pizza.

7. The customers decide to go with a bottle of the house red wine.

8. The waiter assures the customers that he will have their special requests sorted out.

9. The customers express interest in trying the chocolate lava cake for dessert because they are up for it.

10. The customers decide to save room for dessert because it sounds too delicious to pass up.

Affordable Housing

Kerry and Joe are talking about the housing situation in Vancouver.

Kerry: Did you hear that the city of Vancouver is **taking action** to address **housing prices**?

Joe: What are they doing? I'd love to move but **affordable housing** is hard to come by.

Kerry: They're building a new **housing development** and offering **low-interest rate** mortgages.

Joe: **It's about time**. Unless you **inherit money**, it's almost impossible for the **working Joe** to buy a house here.

Kerry: Well, **check into it** and if you buy one, invite me to your **housewarming party**!

Vocabulary

taking action: Doing something.

housing prices: The average price of houses in an area.

affordable housing: Housing that is designed to be cheaper than normal, usually subsidized by the government.

housing development: An area in which the houses have all been planned and built at the same time in an organized way.

low-interest rates: When interest rates are lower than normal.

it's about time: Finally.

inherit money: Getting money after someone has died.

working Joe: The average working person.

check into it: Find out more information about something.

housewarming party: A party after moving into a new home.

Practice

1. What are the average _____ in Victoria like?

2. Are you going to _____ when your parents die?

3. I've love to get into that new _____ in the west end of the city.

4. I'm happy that the city is finally _____ on that guy across the street.

5. There's no _____ in New York City.

6. Congratulations on your new place! When's the _____?

7. Did he finally do his chores? _____.

8. I'm just an average _____, doing the 9-5.

9. I'm not sure about that. I'll have to _____.

10. It's a great time to buy a house when there are _____.

Answers

1. housing prices

2. inherit money

3. housing development

4. taking action

5. affordable housing

6. housewarming party

7. it's about time

8. working Joe

9. check into it

10. low-interest rates

An Introduction to Economics

Economics serves as a comprehensive social science that **probes** the intricate ways in which individuals, businesses, and societies manage and allocate resources to fulfill their **insatiable** wants and needs. This field extends its reach from the intricacies of personal decision-making to the broader spectrum of global economic trends.

The Foundation: Scarcity and Decision-Making

At the heart of economic principles lies the concept of scarcity. This arises due to the inherent limitation of resources such as time, money, and natural assets, **juxtaposed** against the boundless human desires. Consequently, individuals, businesses, and governments must navigate the challenge of making choices and trade-offs to **optimize** resource allocation and achieve their respective objectives.

Microeconomics: Decoding Individual Behavior

Microeconomics, as a foundational **pillar**, concentrates on the behavior of discrete entities such as households, firms, and markets. This branch of economics scrutinizes the decision-making processes of consumers and firms, unraveling the complexities of choices, production, and pricing strategies. Furthermore, microeconomics delves into the nuances of market structures, including perfect competition, monopoly, and oligopoly, which shape the dynamics of supply and demand.

Macroeconomics: A Holistic Perspective

Taking a panoramic view, macroeconomics focuses on the comprehensive performance of an entire economy. Key indicators such as inflation, unemployment, economic growth, and government policies fall under its scrutiny. Macroeconomists seek to comprehend the factors influencing these broad-scale indicators and devise strategies to foster stability and enhancement on a national or global economic scale.

The Market Forces: Supply and Demand Dynamics

Central to economic discourse is the elemental interplay between supply and demand. These twin forces dictate prices and quantities within markets. When demand surpasses supply, prices ascend, incentivizing producers to increase output. Conversely, when supply outstrips demand, prices decline, prompting producers to scale back production. This dynamic equilibrium serves as a fundamental driver of economic transactions.

Government's Role: Policies and Interventions

Beyond market forces, economists investigate the role of governments in shaping economic outcomes. Through policies such as taxation, subsidies, and regulations, governments intervene to address market failures, foster fair competition, and promote societal well-being. Striking the delicate balance between market autonomy and government intervention is a perennial subject of debate in economic theory and policy discussions.

Economic Systems: Capitalism, Socialism, and Beyond

Economic systems, ranging from capitalism to socialism, exert a profound influence on the economic landscape. Capitalist economies emphasize private ownership and free markets, while socialist economies advocate for collective or government ownership and control. The study of economics unveils the strengths and weaknesses inherent in each system, contributing to ongoing discussions about the optimal economic structure.

Conclusion: Empowering Informed Decision-Making

In conclusion, economics provides a robust framework for deciphering the multifaceted decisions and interactions that propel our global society. Equipping individuals with tools to analyze supply and demand, decipher market structures, comprehend government policies, and assess economic systems, the study of economics fosters informed decision-making across personal, business, and policy realms. As we explore the intricate web of economic forces, we gain valuable insights into the mechanisms shaping our world and steering the well-being of individuals and societies.

Vocabulary

scarcity: The fundamental economic concept that refers to the limited availability of resources in comparison to the unlimited human wants and needs.

microeconomics: The branch of economics that focuses on the behaviors and decisions of individual entities such as households, businesses, and markets.

macroeconomics: The study of the overall performance and behavior of an entire economy, examining indicators like inflation, unemployment, and economic growth.

supply and demand: The fundamental forces driving market dynamics, where supply represents the quantity of a good or service available, and demand is the quantity buyers are willing to purchase at a given price.

government intervention: Actions taken by the government in the economy, such as regulations, subsidies, and taxes, to address market failures or promote certain outcomes.

market structures: The different organizational arrangements of markets, including perfect competition, monopoly, and oligopoly, influencing pricing and competition.

inflation: A sustained increase in the general price level of goods and services in an economy, resulting in a decrease in the purchasing power of a currency.

unemployment: The condition where individuals who are willing and able to work are unable to find employment.

capitalism: An economic system characterized by private ownership of resources and the means of production, with a focus on free-market competition.

socialism: An economic system advocating for collective or government ownership and control of the means of production, aiming for more equitable distribution of wealth and resources.

Vocabulary Challenge

1. Probes, in the first paragraph is most closely related to:

   a) space exploration

   b) seeks to uncover information

   c) done in surgery

   d) tries

2. insatiable, in the first paragraph is most closely related to:

   a) thirsty

   b) without end

   c) unable to do something

   d) impossible to satisfy

3. juxtaposed, in the second paragraph is most closely related to:

   a) a visual effect

   b) something social scientists do

   c) related to comparing things

   d) an economic term

4. Optimize, in the second paragraph is most closely related to:

   a) make the best use of something

   b) to begin something

   c) related to sight

   d) to finish something

5. Pillar, in the third paragraph is most closely related to:

a) a strong piece of wood or steel

b) medication

c) something that provides support

d) a support structure for a building

Answers

1. b

2. d

3. c

4. a

5. c

Multiple Choice Questions

1. What is the fundamental economic concept that arises due to the limited availability of resources compared to unlimited human wants and needs?

a. Abundance

b. Wealth

c. Scarcity

d. Surplus

2. Which branch of economics focuses on the behaviors and decisions of individual entities such as households, businesses, and markets?

a. Macroeconomics

b. Microeconomics

c. Econometrics

d. Behavioral Economics

3. What term describes the forces that determine prices and quantities in markets, where supply represents availability and demand reflects consumer desire?

a. Competition

b. Equilibrium

c. Monopoly

d. Inflation

4. In economics, what does the term "inflation" refer to?

a. Decrease in the money supply

b. Rise in the general price level

c. Increase in unemployment

d. Contraction of the economy

5. What does the government often use to address market failures and promote specific economic outcomes?

a. Taxes

b. Subsidies

c. Regulations

d. All of the above

6. Which economic system is characterized by private ownership of resources and a focus on free-market competition?

a. Socialism

b. Capitalism

c. Communism

d. Fascism

7. What is the term for the condition where individuals who are willing and able to work cannot find employment?

a. Underemployment

b. Disemployment

c. Unemployment

d. Overemployment

8. Which economic indicator is concerned with the overall performance and behavior of an entire economy?

a. Microeconomic indicators

b. Inflation rate

c. Unemployment rate

d. Macroeconomic indicators

9. What is the economic term for actions taken by the government in the market, such as setting prices or limiting competition?

a. Market forces

b. Government intervention

c. Price control

d. Market equilibrium

10. What is the study of different organizational arrangements of markets, including perfect competition, monopoly, and oligopoly?

a. Market segmentation

b. Market structures

c. Market equilibrium

d. Market dynamics

Answers

1. c
2. b
3. b
4. b
5. d
6. b
7. c
8. d
9. b
10. b

Famine

Sam and Carrie are talking about a famine.

Sam: Have you heard about the **famine** in ABC country?

Carrie: I have. It seems really bad, but I don't know much about it. Is it an **anomaly** or an **annual** thing?

Sam: Oh, it happens every year. Experts **attribute** it to XYZ country **diverting** and taking a **disproportionate** amount of water from the main river running through both countries.

Carrie: So frustrating and sad. Water shouldn't be a **finite** resource. Of course this would **impoverish** that country if it were happening every single year. We need to **augment** our financial aid to poorer countries.

Vocabulary

famine: Extreme lack of food (usually at the country level).

anomaly: Something that is not the norm.

annual: Occurring yearly.

attribute: Give credit to.

diverting: Change of course.

disproportionate: Too large or too smart compared to something else.

finite: Having an end or limit.

impoverish: To reduce to poverty.

augment: Increase, or make larger.

Practice

1. That _____ has killed hundreds of thousands of people so far.

2. Rich countries use a _____ amount of fossil fuels.

3. We won! It was kind of an _____. A small miracle.

4. The government didn't intend to _____ that whole group of people but that was the effect.

5. We have to stop _____ funds away from advertising. It's short-sighted.

6. Where are you going for your _____girl's trip?

7. We have _____ money. There has to be a way to reduce our budget each month.

8. You didn't come up with this idea on your own. You need to _____ it.

Answers

1. famine

2. disproportionate

3. anomaly

4. impoverish

5. diverting

6. annual

7. finite

8. attribute

The Frog and the Ox

Once upon a time, in a **tranquil** meadow surrounded by swaying wildflowers, a small frog named Freddy lived happily. His daily adventures led him to observe the **massive** ox, Oliver, who grazed nearby. Oliver, the largest and strongest creature in the meadow, commanded respect from all and Freddy greatly **admired** him.

One sunny day, Freddy couldn't help but feel a twinge of envy as he watched Oliver. "If only I were as big as Oliver," he thought. Driven by this desire, Freddy decided to approach Oliver and share his thoughts. **Hopping** over with a cheerful "Hello," Freddy began a conversation with the wise ox.

"Hello, little friend," responded Oliver, lowering his massive head to meet Freddy's gaze. "What brings you here?"

Expressing his longing to be as impressive as Oliver, Freddy shared his feelings. Oliver, with a chuckle, decided to teach Freddy a valuable lesson. He inflated his chest, making himself even larger than usual. However, to everyone's surprise, Oliver's efforts were in vain, and he let out a loud "POP!" The meadow echoed with the sound of escaping air.

Freddy couldn't help but giggle at the sight. "Well, Oliver, it seems that trying to be something you're not doesn't always work."

Oliver nodded, acknowledging Freddy's wisdom. "You're right, Freddy. Embrace who you are and be proud of your unique qualities. Size may impress some, but true greatness comes from being yourself."

From that day forward, Freddy learned to appreciate his small size and the unique details that made him special. The meadow echoed with the laughter of the little frog, who had discovered that being content with oneself was the key to true happiness.

The Moral

The moral of this fable is: "Be happy with who you are and appreciate your own unique qualities. Trying to be someone you're not might not bring the happiness you seek."

Vocabulary

hopping: Jumping.

admired: Looked up to.

mighty: Very large or strong.

massive: Huge.

tranquil: Peaceful and quiet.

Comprehension Questions

1. Why did Freddy, the little frog, approach Oliver, the mighty ox?
2. What did Oliver, the wise ox, do to try to teach Freddy a lesson?
3. What happened when Oliver tried to make himself even larger?
4. What did Freddy learn from the experience with Oliver?
5. What did Freddy realize about true greatness through his encounter with Oliver?

Answers

1. Freddy approached Oliver because he admired the ox's size and strength and wished he could be as impressive.
2. Oliver inflated his chest, making himself even larger than usual, in an attempt to show Freddy the challenges that come with trying to be something you're not.
3. When Oliver inflated his chest, he let out a loud "POP!" as the air escaped, teaching Freddy that trying to be something you're not can have unexpected consequences.
4. Freddy learned to embrace who he was and appreciate his own unique qualities instead of wishing to be someone else.
5. Freddy realized that true greatness comes from being oneself, and it's not necessarily linked to size or outward appearances.

Talking about a Company in Trouble

Jerry is talking to Linda about trouble at his company.

Jerry: My company has been **cutting corners** on this latest project and we're **in hot water**.

Linda: Well, honestly, it's time for your company to **face the music.** You've been doing some things that **cross the line** for years now. It's going to be **an uphill battle** for you.

Jerry: Hey, hey. I know. You're **barking up the wrong tree**! I don't have anything to do with making the decisions. I do what I'm told. I'm basically a **yes man.**

Linda: I know. But, I wish you'd find some **greener pastures**. That company is going to **go under** soon I think. Just **read between the lines**.

Jerry: Well, jobs in my field are like a **needle in a haystack** these days. I'd **pull the plug** if I could.

Vocabulary

cutting Corners: Doing something cheaply or badly. Can often be related to construction/home renovations.

face the music: Deal with the reality of something negative that you did. For example, getting punished for a crime.

in hot water: In trouble for something.

cross the line: Behave in an unacceptable way.

barking up the wrong tree: Blaming someone for something that isn't their fault.

greener pastures: A better opportunity someplace else.

go under: Go bankrupt or out of business.

yes man: A weak person who always agrees with their superior at work or in politics.

needle in a haystack: Something that is impossible to find.

an uphill battle: Something very difficult to deal with.

read between the lines: Discovering something secret or hidden.

pull the plug: Quit, or stop doing something.

Practice

1. That CEO made some terrible decisions and his company is about to _____.

2. I know you don't want to _____ but your company is about to go bankrupt.

3. I'm leaving my job and heading for _____.

4. It's time to _____ for ripping all those customers off.

5. Honestly, you're _____. Johnny did it, not me.

6. Donald Trump is _____ these days with the most recent scandal.

7. The guy painting my house is _____. I feel so angry about it.

8. I hate that my company likes to _____ on just about every deal they do.

9. I hate that my husband is forced into being a _____ in his new role at the company.

10. Looking for my glasses in my messy house is like finding a _____.

11. Quite honestly, it's going to be _____ to get back on track.

12. I think he's going to _____. That new guy just isn't performing well.

Answers

1. go under

2. read between the lines

3. greener pastures

4. face the music

5. barking up the wrong tree

6. in hot water

7. cutting corners

8. cross the line

9. yes man

10. needle in a haystack

11. an uphill battle

12. pull the plug

Flying for the First Time

Someone is nervous about his first time flying on a plane.

Passenger: Hi there! I've never flown before, and I'm a bit nervous. Any tips for this first-timer?

Flight Attendant: Hey! No worries at all. You'll be just fine. First off, make sure to **check in** online before arriving at the airport. It'll save you some time.

Passenger: Got it! And when I'm at the gate, what should I do?

Flight Attendant: When they call for boarding, have your boarding pass and ID ready. It'll help things move smoothly. Once on board, find your seat, and feel free to **settle in**.

Passenger: Okay, that sounds manageable. What if I get hungry during the flight?

Flight Attendant: We'll **come around** with the food and beverage cart. You can **pick out** something you like from the menu. If you need anything, just **flag us down**.

Passenger: Great! And what about turbulence? I heard it can be a bit unsettling.

Flight Attendant: True, it can be a bit bumpy at times. Just stay seated and **buckle up** when the seatbelt sign is on. It helps ensure everyone's safety.

Passenger: Thanks for the heads up! What if I need to use the restroom?

Flight Attendant: No problem! You can **head back** to the restroom at any time. Just be aware of the seatbelt sign, and wait until it's off before getting up.

Passenger: Perfect! Anything else I should know for a smooth flight?

Flight Attendant: Just **lean back** in your seat, relax, and enjoy the journey. If you have any questions or concerns, feel free to **reach out to** one of the flight attendants.

Vocabulary

check in: to register one's arrival, especially at an airport, by obtaining a boarding pass and confirming details.

settle in: to arrange oneself comfortably in a seat or place, often for an extended period.

come around: to move through an area or pass by, in this context, referring to the flight attendants with the food and beverage cart.

pick out: to choose or select, often from a variety of options.

flag down: to attract attention, typically by waving one's hand or signaling.

buckle up: to fasten one's seatbelt, usually in response to safety instructions or when the seatbelt sign is on.

head back: to move toward the rear or back part of the aircraft.

lean back: to recline or move one's seat backward, typically for relaxation.

reach out to: to make contact or communicate with someone, often for assistance or information.

Phrasal Verb Challenge

Fill in the blanks with the appropriate phrasal verbs:

1. Before your flight, make sure to _____ online to save time at the airport.

2. Once on the plane, find your seat and _____ for the journey ahead.

3. The flight attendants will _____ with the food and beverage cart shortly.

4. Feel free to _____ a movie or music from the in-flight entertainment options.

5. If you need assistance during the flight, don't hesitate to _____ a flight attendant.

6. Remember to _____ when the seatbelt sign is on for your safety.

7. If you need to use the restroom, you can _____ to the rear of the aircraft.

8. After a meal, you might want to _____ and relax for a while.

9. If you have questions or concerns, feel free to _____ the airline's customer service.

10. When landing, ensure you _____ your seatbelt until the aircraft comes to a complete stop.

Answers

1. check in
2. settle in
3. come around
4. pick out
5. reach out to
6. buckle up
7. head back
8. lean back
9. reach out to
10. buckle up

Comprehension Questions

1. How does the passenger plan to save time at the airport before the flight?
2. What advice does the flight attendant give regarding boarding?
3. What does the flight attendant suggest the passenger do once on the plane?
4. How does the flight attendant describe the process of serving food and beverages during the flight?
5. What does the flight attendant recommend the passenger do if they want to watch a movie during the flight?
6. How can the passenger get the attention of a flight attendant if they need assistance?
7. When should the passenger buckle up according to the flight attendant's instructions?
8. What is the flight attendant's suggestion if the passenger needs to use the restroom during the flight?
9. What does the flight attendant advise the passenger to do after a meal?
10. In what situations does the flight attendant suggest the passenger reach out to the airline's customer service?

Answers

1. The passenger plans to save time at the airport by checking in online before the flight.
2. The flight attendant advises having the boarding pass and ID ready when they call for boarding.
3. The flight attendant suggests the passenger settle in once on the plane.
4. The flight attendant describes coming around with the food and beverage cart during the flight.
5. The flight attendant recommends the passenger pick out a movie or music from the in-flight entertainment options.
6. To get the attention of a flight attendant, the passenger can flag them down.
7. The passenger should buckle up when the seatbelt sign is on, according to the flight attendant's instructions.
8. If the passenger needs to use the restroom during the flight, they can head back to the rear of the aircraft.
9. After a meal, the flight attendant suggests the passenger lean back and relax for a while.
10. The flight attendant advises the passenger to reach out to the airline's customer service if they have questions or concerns.

Dumped

Alex got dumped by his girlfriend.

John: Hey **bro**, what's up? You don't look so good.

Alex: I just got **dumped** by Kendra. And just when we started talking about **getting hitched.**

John: Sorry to hear that. Wasn't she super **flakey** though, always cancelling at the last minute?

Alex: Yeah, and I **straight up** caught her lying to me more than a few times.

John: Better off without her. Let's get **ripped** this weekend. It'll take your mind off of it.

Alex: Yeah, I want to **blow off some steam**. Just don't post about it on social media. I don't want to get **busted** by my boss. He just **added me** as a friend on Facebook.

Vocabulary

bro: A way to greet a close male friend (if you're also a guy).

dumped: Broken up with.

getting hitched: Getting married.

flakey: Describes someone who doesn't follow through with what they say or always cancels plans.

straight up: Speaking honestly.

ripped: Drunk.

blow off some steam: Relax; let loose.

added me: Becoming friends with someone on social media.

Practice

1. What do you like to do to _____?

2. I'll never work on another project with her if I can avoid it. She's so _____.

3. I got _____ last night at the work Christmas party. I hope that I didn't do anything too embarrassing.

4. Did you hear that Ted _____ Lindsay?

5. My grandma just _____ on Instagram. It's so cute!

6. I _____ never want to talk to that guy again.

7. Tom and I are _____ next month.

8. Hey _____, how are you doing these days?

Answers

1. blow off some steam

2. flakey

3. ripped

4. dumped

5. added me

6. straight up

7. getting hitched

8. bro

An Introduction to Music

Music, a universal language that transcends cultural and linguistic boundaries, has been an **integral** part of the human experience throughout history. From the rhythmic beats of ancient drums to the intricate compositions of classical symphonies and the **vibrant** melodies of contemporary genres, music reflects and shapes the diverse **tapestry** of human emotions, cultures, and societies.

The Essence of Music: A Harmonious Blend of Elements

At its core, music is an art form that involves the organized arrangement of sounds and silence. It encompasses a vast **spectrum** of styles, genres, and traditions, each offering a unique lens through which to explore and appreciate the expressive potential of sound. Whether instrumental or vocal, music has the power to **evoke** powerful emotions, tell stories, and convey complex messages without the need for words.

Rhythm: The Heartbeat of Music

One of the fundamental elements of music is rhythm, the pattern of beats and durations that provides a sense of order and structure. Rhythm is the heartbeat of music, setting the pace and creating a foundation for the other musical elements to unfold. Whether it's the steady thump of a bass drum in a rock song, the syncopated rhythms of jazz, or the intricate patterns of a tabla in Indian classical music, rhythm plays a crucial role in shaping the character and feel of a musical piece.

Melody: Crafting Memorable Tunes

Melody, another essential component of music, consists of a sequence of pitches that create a memorable and recognizable tune. Melodies can be simple or complex, ranging from the familiar tunes of nursery rhymes to the intricate and emotive lines of a violin concerto. The interplay of melodies and harmonies, the combination of different pitches played simultaneously, adds depth and richness to musical compositions.

Harmony: The Art of Sonic Texture

Harmony, the simultaneous combination of different musical notes, contributes to the texture and color of a musical piece. Whether it's the harmonious chords of a choir, the intricate interplay of instruments in an orchestra, or the dissonant tones of experimental music, harmony shapes the overall sonic landscape, creating a sense of tension or resolution.

Cultural Significance: Music as a Reflection of Society

In addition to these structural elements, music is deeply connected to cultural, social, and historical contexts. Different cultures and societies have developed their own unique musical traditions, instruments, and styles, reflecting the values, beliefs, and experiences of their communities. From the traditional folk music of a specific region to the global influence of contemporary pop and electronic music, the diversity of musical expression is a testament to the richness of human creativity.

Expressive Power: Music as Personal and Collective Expression

Music also serves as a vehicle for personal and collective expression. Artists use music to convey their emotions, tell stories, and comment on social and political issues. Whether it's the protest songs of the 1960s, the anthems that define cultural movements, or the introspective lyrics of a singer-songwriter, music has the power to inspire, provoke thought, and unite people across different backgrounds.

Evolution of Music: Technological Advancements and Global Connectivity

As technology has advanced, the ways in which we create, consume, and share music have evolved. The advent of recording technology, radio, and streaming platforms has democratized access to music, allowing artists to reach global audiences and listeners to explore a vast array of musical genres. This interconnectedness has fueled innovation and cross-cultural influences, shaping the ever-changing landscape of the music industry.

Conclusion: Music as an Essential and Enduring Human Experience

In conclusion, the world of music is a vast thing that encompasses an array of styles, traditions, and expressions. It is a powerful form of communication that has been an integral part of human history and continues to evolve in response to cultural, technological, and societal changes. Whether experienced in a concert hall or through headphones, music has the ability to inspire, move, and connect people on a profound level, making it an essential and enduring aspect of the human experience.

Vocabulary

harmony: The simultaneous combination of different musical notes to create a pleasing and balanced sound.

rhythm: The pattern of beats and durations in music, providing a sense of time and structure.

melody: A sequence of musical notes that forms a tune and is often the most memorable part of a piece.

genre: A category or style of music characterized by distinctive features, such as rock, jazz, or classical.

composition: A piece of music created by arranging and organizing musical elements like melody, harmony, and rhythm.

tempo: The speed at which a piece of music is played, influencing its mood and overall feel.

crescendo: A gradual increase in volume or intensity in a musical piece.

dynamics: The variation in loudness and intensity in music, contributing to its expressive qualities.

lyrics: The words or text of a song, often expressing emotions, stories, or messages.

instrumentation: The selection and arrangement of instruments in a musical composition or performance.

Vocabulary Challenge

1. Integral, in the first paragraph is closest in meaning to:

   a) necessary

   b) unimportant

   c) a mathematical term

   d) the most important thing

2. Vibrant, in the first paragraph is most closely related to:

   a) describes a bright color

   b) quivering

   c) dull

   d) full of energy

3. Tapestry, in the first paragraph is most closely related to:

   a) a decorative piece of cloth

   b) a collection

   c) describes a single thing

   d) a window covering

4. Spectrum, in in the second paragraph is most closely related to:

   a) various colors

   b) related to autism

   c) related to sound and particles

   d) a range

5. Evoke, in the second paragraph is most closely related to:

   a) bringing to the consciousness

   b) call on the spirits

   c) elicit a response

   d) move from one place to another

Answers

1. a

2. d

3. b

4. d

5. c

Multiple Choice Questions

1. What is the term for the simultaneous combination of different musical notes, contributing to the texture and color of a musical piece?

   a. Melody

   b. Harmony

   c. Rhythm

   d. Tempo

2. In music, what is the pattern of beats and durations that provides a sense of time and structure?

   a. Melody

   b. Harmony

   c. Rhythm

   d. Crescendo

3. Which term refers to a gradual increase in volume or intensity in a musical piece?

   a. Dynamics

   b. Crescendo

   c. Tempo

   d. Composition

4. What is the category or style of music characterized by distinctive features, such as rock, jazz, or classical?

 a. Melody

 b. Genre

 c. Harmony

 d. Composition

5. What is a sequence of musical notes that forms a tune and is often the most memorable part of a piece?

 a. Harmony

 b. Crescendo

 c. Melody

 d. Tempo

6. What term is used to describe the speed at which a piece of music is played, influencing its mood and overall feel?

 a. Crescendo

 b. Dynamics

 c. Tempo

 d. Genre

7. Which term refers to the variation in loudness and intensity in music, contributing to its expressive qualities?

 a. Tempo

 b. Dynamics

 c. Rhythm

 d. Composition

8. What are the words or text of a song, often expressing emotions, stories, or messages?

   a. Lyrics

   b. Harmony

   c. Instrumentation

   d. Crescendo

9. What is the term for the arrangement of instruments in a musical composition or performance?

   a. Tempo

   b. Dynamics

   c. Instrumentation

   d. Melody

10. What is a piece of music created by arranging and organizing musical elements like melody, harmony, and rhythm?

   a. Composition

   b. Genre

   c. Crescendo

   d. Lyrics

Answers

1. b
2. c
3. b
4. b
5. c
6. c
7. b
8. a
9. c
10. a

Finishing Work for the Day

Jerry and Linda are going to get some dinner after work.

Jerry: I'm so tired. Let's **call it a day** and grab some dinner. It's **my treat**.

Linda: Sure, I'd love to but only if we **go Dutch**. You **foot the bill** for me too often!

Jerry: Sure, if you insist. Let's check out that dessert place. They have sandwiches and then I can satisfy my **sweet tooth**. It's expensive but **worth it** I think.

Linda: Okay, **twist my arm**. Let's go. And don't just pick up the bill when I'm in the bathroom. I want to **pony up** for my share, okay?

Jerry: Let's **make a break for it** before **the big cheese** finds more work for us to do!

Linda: Sure, let's **head out.**

Vocabulary

call it a day: To stop working for the rest of the day.

foot the bill: To pay for.

go Dutch: Each person pays their own bill, especially at a restaurant or bar.

pony up: To get money/credit cards out to pay for something.

worth it: Good enough to justify the high cost.

twist my arm: Convince to do something.

sweet tooth: To like sugary foods.

my treat: To offer to pay, usually for a meal or drink.

make a break for it: Leave somewhere quickly.

the big cheese: The boss.

head out: To go somewhere.

Practice

1. I feel uncomfortable when guys pay for me so I insist that we _____.

2. It's time to _____ for all those drinks you had!

3. I have a wicked _____ and can't stop eating candy.

4. Is the company going to _____ for the Christmas party this year?

5. Let's _____. I'm beat.

6. It's time to _____ and go home while the boss isn't looking.

7. Let's grab lunch. _____.

8. I hope to be _____ one day!

9. I'm tired. I'm going to _____ now.

10. Okay, I know that subscription box is expensive but it's _____ to me.

11. I didn't want to do it! My wife had to _____ to get me to go skydiving with her.

Answers

1. go Dutch

2. pony up

3. sweet tooth

4. foot the bill

5. call it a day

6. make a break for it

7. my treat

8. the big cheese

9. head out

10. worth it

11. twist my arm

Idioms #6

Let the cat out of the bag

Meaning: To reveal a secret, on purpose or unintentionally.

Origin: Refers to the "cat o-nine tails." It's a whipping device (with nine cords) that is used to punish sailors. In the bag refers to the leather nature of the device because it has to be stored in a bag to prevent it from drying out.

"Jen! I can't believe you *let the cat out of the bag*. I'm so disappointed in you."

"Oh, I'm so sorry. I *let the cat out of the bag*. I didn't know that it was a secret."

Let the dust settle

Meaning: Wait for and let a situation become calm or normal after something exciting or unusual happened. Give something time before proceeding.

Origin: Unknown. But, could be related to construction where there's lots of dust that needs to settle before a place is inhabitable.

"I think we should *let the dust settle* before deciding on this."

"I'm not sure what the result will be. We need to *let the dust settle* first."

Lighten up

Meaning: Relax, chill out; don't take things so seriously.

Origin: Earlier forms date from around 1400. Could be related to the weighing of the heart after death. If it's light (with good deeds), it goes up to Heaven. If it's too heavy (with bad deeds), it goes down to Hell.

"Hey! *Lighten up*. I was only joking."

"My teacher needs to *lighten up*. It's like he tries to never laugh."

Love is blind

Meaning: To imply that with love, one is unable to see the faults or imperfections of a person. It can also mean that the looks of a person do not matter when you're in love.

Origin: First appeared in the early 1400s and was popularized by Shakespeare's works.

"Just go on a date with him. He's such a nice guy and *love is blind*, right?"

"*Love is blind* must be working for Craig. I can't believe Tina married him."

Mad as a hatter

Meaning: To be completely crazy.

Origin: From the 1600s when hat makers used to use mercury in their felt hats. This resulted in people getting sick and appearing to be crazy.

"Are you *as mad as a hatter*? Tammy will never agree to go on a date with you!"

"You kids! You're *as mad as hatters*. I won't make you an ice cream sundae until after you clean your room."

Make a show out of (something)

Meaning: To do something in a way that attracts attention.

Origin: Uncertain.

"Stop m*aking a show out of cooking dinner*. You know that I do it almost every night and don't make a big deal out of it, right?"

"Toby *makes such a show out of doing the laundry*. It's so annoying. Who does he think does laundry the other 90% of the time?"

My neck of the woods

Meaning: The area where I/he/she/they live.

Origin: Uncertain.

"We can play tennis in *your neck of the woods next time*."

The Ant and the Grasshopper

In a bustling meadow, there lived two neighbors – an ant named Andy and a **carefree** grasshopper named Greg. They were different from each other in their attitudes towards life.

Andy, the ant, was diligent and hardworking. He spent his days collecting and **storing** food and building a sturdy anthill to prepare for winter. Greg, the grasshopper, loved to hop around, play his cheerful tunes, and enjoy the warm sunshine without a care in the world.

As the days turned cooler, Andy continued to work **tirelessly**, storing food and reinforcing his anthill. Greg, however, continued to sing and dance, believing that the good times would never end.

One day, a chill filled the air, and dark clouds gathered in the sky. Winter was **approaching**. Andy had more than enough food stored to survive the cold months ahead a and he **thrived.** Meanwhile, Greg found himself hungry and **shivering**, realizing he hadn't prepared for the harsh winter.

Desperate and cold, Greg approached Andy's anthill and humbly asked, "Andy, could you spare some food? I didn't plan for winter, and now I'm in need." Andy looked at Greg with a mix of sympathy and disappointment. "I warned you to prepare, Greg. Now, I must focus on my own survival," he replied.

Realizing his mistake, Greg felt a pang of regret. He had spent the warm months playing and not thinking about the future. Now, he had to face the consequences of his actions.

As winter set in, Andy stayed warm and well-fed in his cozy anthill, while Greg struggled in the cold. The once carefree grasshopper learned the importance of planning and hard work the hard way.

The story of Andy, the industrious ant, and Greg, the carefree grasshopper, teaches us that preparation and hard work lead to success, while negligence can result in hardship. It's a valuable lesson about the importance of planning for the future.

The Moral

The moral of the story is: "It's important to work hard and plan for the future so that you can be prepared for tough times."

Vocabulary

storing: Keeping for future use.

carefree: Without worry.

thrived: Did well.

approached: Got nearer.

shivering: Shaking a little bit due to cold.

Comprehension Questions

1. Who were the two friends in the story?
2. What did Andy do to prepare for winter?
3. How did Greg spend his time while Andy was preparing for winter?
4. When winter arrived, how did Andy and Greg do?
5. What is the moral of the story?

Answers

1. The two friends in the story were Andy, the hardworking ant, and Greg, the playful grasshopper.
2. Andy worked hard, storing food for winter, and reinforcing his anthill.
3. Greg spent his time playing, not making preparations for winter.
4. Andy thrived in winter because he had stored enough food and made preparations. Greg struggled because he hadn't planned for the cold season.
5. The moral of the story is that it's important to work hard and plan for the future.

The Chicken or the Egg

Bob and Sam are talking about Sam's son.

Bob: Hey, how's your son doing these days? I heard he got into a bit of trouble?

Sam: He **drives me up the wall**. He's both a **slacker** and a **stoner.** I don't know if it's **the chicken or the egg** but whatever the case, he's **flunking** out of high school because he's always **high**.

Bob: You were such a **keener** in school. How did this happen?

Sam: Trust me. I have no idea.

Bob: What does he say when you talk to him?

Sam: He just yells, "**Get off my back**!" We can't even have a real conversation about it. I'm scared he's ruining his life.

Bob: Well, I'm here for you if you need to talk about things.

Vocabulary

drives me up the wall: Makes me crazy.

slacker: Describes someone who is lazy.

stoner: Describes someone who likes to do illegal drugs often.

the chicken or the egg: Which thing comes first?

flunking: Failing.

high: On drugs.

keener: Describes someone who is the opposite of lazy.

get off my back: Stop bugging me.

Practice

1. Seriously, _____. I don't want to talk about this anymore.

2. It _____ when he doesn't put his dishes in the dishwasher.

3. You're such a _____, studying two weeks before the test.

4. Is it _____? It's difficult to tell in this situation.

5. Let's get _____ after work tonight.

6. I was a _____ in high school but I quit when I went to university.

7. I'm _____ math but I don't care.

8. My daughter is a _____ and doesn't care about school. She'd rather just hang around with her friends.

Answers

1. get off my back

2. drives me up the wall

3. keener

4. the chicken or the egg

5. high

6. stoner

7. flunking

8. slacker

Checking Into a Hotel

Someone is checking into a hotel.

Receptionist: Good evening! How can I assist you today?

Guest: Hi! I'd like to **check in**, please. I've already booked a room online.

Receptionist: Great! Could you please provide your ID and the credit card you used for the reservation?

Guest: Sure, here you go. Do I need to **fill out** any forms?

Receptionist: No need for that. I've already **pulled up** your reservation. Let me just verify some details. It'll only take a moment.

Guest: Take your time. By the way, what time can I expect my room to be ready?

Receptionist: Your room is already prepared. You can go ahead and **settle in**. The elevator is right over there.

Guest: Thanks! Oh, and can you recommend any good places to grab a quick bite around here?

Receptionist: Certainly! There's a nice café just around the corner. You might want to **check out**. They serve delicious pastries.

Guest: Sounds perfect! I'll definitely check it out. By the way, is there someone I can **reach out to** if I need extra towels or anything else during my stay?

Receptionist: Absolutely! Feel free to dial "0" from your room phone. Our staff will be happy to **assist with** any requests you may have.

Guest: Excellent, thanks for the info. I'll **head up** to my room now and **get settled**.

Vocabulary

check in: To register one's arrival, especially at a hotel, by providing necessary information and obtaining room keys.

fill out: To complete a form or document by providing required information.

pulled up: To retrieve or access information from a database or system.

settle in: To make oneself comfortable in a new place or situation, often by unpacking and arranging personal belongings.

reach out to: To make contact or communicate with someone for assistance or information.

head up: To go or move towards a higher level or destination.

get settled: To arrange oneself comfortably, often in a new environment or situation.

assist with: To provide help or support in completing a task or fulfilling a request.

Phrasal Verb Challenge

Fill in the blanks with the appropriate phrasal verbs:

1. Upon arriving at the hotel, make sure to _____ at the front desk.

2. Before you leave, please _____ this feedback form to let us know about your stay.

3. The receptionist quickly _____ your reservation details when you provided your name.

4. Once you're in your room, take your time to _____, unpack, and relax.

5. If you have any questions or concerns during your stay, don't hesitate to _____ the hotel staff.

6. If you need additional pillows or amenities, feel free to _____ the hotel concierge.

7. As a guest, you can always _____ the hotel management if you have specific requests.

8. After a long journey, it's essential to _____ and make yourself at home in the hotel room.

9. The hotel staff is more than happy to _____ arranging transportation or providing local information.

10. If you require any assistance with your luggage, the bellhop can _____ carrying it to your room.

Answers

1. Upon arriving at the hotel, make sure to check in at the front desk.

2. Before you leave, please fill out this feedback form to let us know about your stay.

3. The receptionist quickly pulled up your reservation details when you provided your name.

4. Once you're in your room, take your time to settle in, unpack, and relax.

5. If you have any questions or concerns during your stay, don't hesitate to reach out to the hotel staff.

6. If you need additional pillows or amenities, feel free to assist with the hotel concierge.

7. As a guest, you can always reach out to the hotel management if you have specific requests.

8. After a long journey, it's essential to get settled and make yourself at home in the hotel room.

9. The hotel staff is more than happy to assist with arranging transportation or providing local information.

10. If you require any assistance with your luggage, the bellhop can help with carrying it to your room.

Comprehension Questions

1. What is the guest's primary purpose for approaching the receptionist?

2. How does the guest plan to provide feedback about their stay?

3. In what situation does the receptionist pull up information during the conversation?

4. What advice does the receptionist give to the guest regarding settling into their room?

5. How does the receptionist encourage the guest to seek assistance during their stay?

6. What specific services does the hotel concierge offer, according to the dialogue?

7. When can a guest reach out to the hotel management?

8. What does the guest prioritize upon entering their hotel room?

9. How does the hotel staff express their willingness to assist with various aspects of the guest's stay?

10. What additional service does the bellhop offer to the guest?

Answers

1. The guest's primary purpose for approaching the receptionist is to check in at the front desk.

2. The guest plans to provide feedback about their stay by filling out a feedback form before leaving.

3. The receptionist pulls up information when the guest provides their name to check in.

4. The receptionist advises the guest to take their time to settle in, unpack, and relax in their room.

5. The receptionist encourages the guest to reach out to the hotel staff if they have any questions or concerns during their stay.

6. The hotel concierge offers to assist with additional pillows or amenities, as mentioned in the conversation.

7. A guest can reach out to the hotel management if they have specific requests, as mentioned in the dialogue.

8. Upon entering their hotel room, the guest prioritizes getting settled and making themselves at home.

9. The hotel staff expresses their willingness to assist with arranging transportation or providing local information.

10. The bellhop offers to help with carrying the guest's luggage to their room.

Break a Leg

Linda is talking to Jerry about a play that she'll be in next month.

Jerry: Hey, I heard **through the grapevine** that you're going to be in a play next month.

Linda: It's true. I must admit! I had to **blow off some steam** from work and escaping into my character is a great way to do that.

Jerry: You're really **taking the bull by the horns** lately! Can I come watch?

Linda: Sure, **knock yourself out**! It's a little bit **amateur hour** but **on the upside**, the tickets are cheap!

Jerry: Okay, I'll come for sure. I can't forget to tell you to **break a leg** though!

Vocabulary

break a leg: To wish someone good luck, usually before performing or going on stage.

blow off some steam: Doing something to get rid of stress. For example, having a few drinks after a difficult work project.

knock yourself out: To try hard to do something. Often something that others think is a waste of time.

taking the bull by the horns: Doing something bravely and decisively.

through the grapevine: To spread information informally. Often related to gossip.

amateur hour: Not professional.

on the upside: Something positive in a generally negative situation.

Practice

1. I heard _____ that Tom and Monica broke up.

2. You want to do that for me? _____.

3. I starting playing soccer to _____ from my terrible job.

4. Well, _____, this job has better hours.

5. Good luck and _____.

6. It was hard to watch that presentation. Talk about _____.

7. I'm _____ at work lately and it's going well!

Answers

1. through the grapevine

2. Knock yourself out

3. blow off some steam

4. on the upside

5. break a leg

6. amateur hour

7. taking the bull by the horns

An Introduction to Medicine

Medicine, a field as **ancient** as human civilization itself, is a dynamic and ever-evolving discipline that encompasses the study, diagnosis, treatment, and prevention of diseases. Rooted in a rich history of scientific inquiry and guided by ethical principles, medicine plays a pivotal role in safeguarding and enhancing human health. The journey of medicine from ancient healing practices to cutting-edge technologies reflects the **ceaseless** pursuit of understanding the complexities of the human body and the relentless quest for innovative solutions to health challenges.

Historical Foundations: From Ancient Healing to Modern Medicine

The origins of medicine can be traced back to ancient civilizations where healers relied on a blend of empirical observations, folklore, and spiritual beliefs to address **ailments**. Ancient Egyptian, Greek, Indian, and Chinese civilizations made significant contributions to early medical knowledge, laying the groundwork for the systematic study of the human body and its functions. Hippocrates, often regarded as the father of Western medicine, introduced a scientific approach to healing, emphasizing observation and documentation.

The Renaissance marked a revival of scientific inquiry and a renewed interest in anatomy and physiology. Visionaries like Andreas Vesalius challenged age-old beliefs, pioneering dissections to gain a deeper understanding of the human body's structure. This period laid the foundation for the scientific method, setting the stage for the systematic and evidence-based practice of medicine that we recognize today.

The Evolution of Medical Education and Practice

Advancements in medical education and the professionalization of medicine further propelled the field forward. The establishment of medical schools and the formal training of physicians became integral to ensuring a standardized and comprehensive approach to healthcare. The 19th and 20th centuries witnessed **groundbreaking** discoveries, such as the germ theory of disease, vaccination, and the development of antibiotics, revolutionizing the treatment and prevention of infections.

As medicine progressed, specialization emerged, with physicians focusing on **specific** organ systems or disease categories. This specialization allowed for in-depth expertise and improved patient outcomes. Concurrently, interdisciplinary collaboration became a hallmark of modern healthcare, bringing together physicians, nurses, pharmacists, and other healthcare professionals to provide holistic and patient-centered care.

Medical Ethics: The Moral Compass of Healthcare

Embedded within the practice of medicine is a commitment to ethical principles that guide the interactions between healthcare providers and patients. The Hippocratic Oath, a foundational ethical code for physicians, underscores the importance of beneficence, non-maleficence, autonomy, and justice in medical practice. Medical ethics addresses dilemmas arising from technological advancements, cultural diversity, and the balancing of individual and societal interests.

Technological Revolution: Innovations Shaping Modern Medicine

The 21st century has ushered in a technological revolution that is transforming the landscape of medicine. From genomics and precision medicine to artificial intelligence and telemedicine, cutting-edge technologies are enhancing diagnostic accuracy, treatment efficacy, and patient care. Personalized medicine tailors treatments to an individual's unique genetic makeup, offering the potential for more targeted and effective interventions.

Telemedicine has expanded access to healthcare, allowing patients to consult with healthcare professionals remotely. Mobile health applications, wearable devices, and health informatics are empowering individuals to actively engage in managing their health. The integration of big data analytics is revolutionizing medical research, enabling the identification of patterns and trends that can inform public health strategies and medical interventions.

Global Health Challenges: Navigating the Complexities

Medicine is not confined to the realms of individual health but extends to addressing global health challenges. Infectious diseases, non-communicable diseases, and health disparities pose complex issues that require international collaboration and innovative solutions. Public health initiatives, vaccination campaigns, and advocacy for equitable access to healthcare resources are crucial components of the global health agenda.

Conclusion: The Ongoing Quest for Health and Healing

In conclusion, medicine stands at the intersection of scientific discovery, ethical principles, and technological innovation. From ancient healing practices to the frontiers of genomics and artificial intelligence, the field has continually adapted to meet the evolving needs of humanity. As medicine continues its journey into the future, the commitment to advancing health, alleviating suffering, and promoting well-being remains unwavering. The intricate tapestry of medicine weaves together a legacy of healing, discovery, and compassion, embodying the enduring human quest for health and healing.

Vocabulary

medicine: The field of study and practice concerned with the diagnosis, treatment, and prevention of diseases to maintain or restore health.

diagnosis: The process of determining the nature and cause of a medical condition or disease through examination, observation, and testing.

treatment: The application of medical interventions, therapies, or procedures to manage, alleviate, or cure a health condition.

prevention: Measures and actions taken to avoid the occurrence or development of diseases, often through lifestyle changes, vaccinations, and public health initiatives.

ethics: The principles and moral guidelines governing the conduct of healthcare professionals, emphasizing values such as integrity, beneficence, and respect for patients' autonomy.

specialization: The focus on a specific area of medicine or healthcare, allowing practitioners to develop expertise in a particular field, such as cardiology or neurology.

genomics: The study of an organism's complete set of genes (genome), including their structure, function, and interaction, with implications for personalized medicine.

telemedicine: The use of technology, such as video calls and remote monitoring, to provide medical care and consultations at a distance.

precision medicine: An approach to healthcare that customizes medical treatment and interventions based on individual characteristics, including genetic makeup, lifestyle, and environmental factors.

global health: The study and promotion of health and well-being on a global scale, addressing health issues that transcend national borders and require international cooperation.

Vocabulary Challenge

1. Ancient, in the first paragraph is most closely related to:

   a) something very old

   b) showing signs of wear and tear

   c) an old person

   d) something no longer in existence

2. Ceaseless, in the first paragraph is most closely related to:

   a) wait

   b) to stop

   c) continuing

   d) never ending

3. Ailments, in the second paragraph is most closely related to:

   a) related to drinking alcohol

   b) an illness you will die from

   c) an illness

   d) a treatment for an illness

4. Groundbreaking, in the fourth paragraph is most closely related to:

   a) to dig

   b) innovative

   c) gathering information about something

   d) to find something

5. Specific, in the fifth paragraph is most closely related to:

   a) clearly defined

   b) a medical treatment

   c) related to a species

   d) denotes a volume

Answers

   1. a

   2. d

   3. c

   4. b

   5. a

213

Multiple Choice Questions

1. What is the primary focus of medicine?

   a. Engineering

   b. Diagnosis, treatment, and prevention of diseases

   c. Agriculture

   d. Astronomy

2. What term refers to the process of determining the nature and cause of a medical condition?

   a. Prognosis

   b. Diagnosis

   c. Prescription

   d. Treatment

3. What are measures taken to avoid the occurrence or development of diseases?

   a. Treatment

   b. Intervention

   c. Prevention

   d. Diagnostics

4. Which term describes the principles and moral guidelines governing the conduct of healthcare professionals?

   a. Laws

   b. Regulations

   c. Ethics

   d. Morals

5. What does the term "genomics" refer to in the context of medicine?

   a. Study of the Earth

   b. Study of genes and their functions

   c. Study of infectious diseases

   d. Study of ancient civilizations

6. What is the practice of providing medical care and consultations at a distance using technology called?

   a. Digital healthcare

   b. Telemedicine

   c. Virtual reality medicine

   d. Cybernetic healthcare

7. What is the concept of customizing medical treatment based on individual characteristics, including genetic makeup?

   a. Holistic medicine

   b. Precision medicine

   c. Alternative medicine

   d. Experimental medicine

8. What is the field of study that focuses on a specific area of medicine, allowing practitioners to develop expertise?

   a. General practice

   b. Specialization

   c. Multidisciplinary medicine

   d. Comprehensive care

9. Which term refers to the complete set of genes in an organism, including their structure, function, and interaction?

    a. Genetics

    b. Genome

    c. Genotype

    d. Genitalia

10. What is the study and promotion of health on a global scale, addressing health issues that transcend national borders?

    a. National Health

    b. International Healthcare

    c. Global Health

    d. Public Health

Answers

    1. b

    2. b

    3. c

    4. c

    5. b

    6. b

    7. b

    8. b

    9. b

    10. c

Lifestyle Changes

Kim is talking to Tanya about her health.

Kim: Did you **go to the doctor**? I know you were **not feeling well**.

Tanya: I did. She didn't **diagnose me** with anything but said that I'd need to make some serious **lifestyle changes**. My **overall health** is quite poor.

Kim: Oh no! What did she recommend?

Tanya: She said that I have to **reduce my stress**, **get plenty of sleep**, and **eat a balanced diet**.

Kim: That doesn't sound so bad. Do you have to **quit smoking**?

Tanya: Oh yeah, that too. It **shook me up**. She said that if I didn't change, my **life expectancy** would decrease.

Vocabulary

go to the doctor: Have an appointment with a doctor.

not feeling well: Feeling sick.

diagnose me: Assign a name to a health problem.

lifestyle changes: Change in what you eat, how much you exercise and other unhealthy habits like smoking or drinking alcohol.

overall health: General level of healthiness/unhealthiness.

reduce my stress: Decrease the amount of stress in your life.

get plenty of sleep: Sleep eight hours a night.

eat a balanced diet: Eating mostly healthy food from all the food groups.

quit smoking: Stop using cigarettes.

shook me up: Made me feel nervous, worried, or anxious.

life expectancy: How long you can expect to live.

Practice

1. In Canada, the average _____ for men is 84 years.

2. Please _____. It seems like you've been sick for a while now.

3. You'll have to make some _____ to reduce your chance of a heart attack.

4. It _____ when he told me that he wanted to get divorced.

5. I'm _____. I need to go home early today.

6. I hope that I can _____ by changing jobs.

7. My goal is to _____ this year but I know it won't be easy.

8. Please try to _____ if you want to lower your cholesterol.

9. My doctor didn't _____ with anything but just said that I had to stop drinking so much coffee.

10. His _____ is quite good, considering how old he is.

11. Please try to _____ before your exam. You'll be able to think more clearly.

Answers

1. life expectancy

2. go to the doctor

3. lifestyle changes

4. shook me up

5. not feeling well

6. reduce my stress

7. quit smoking

8. eat a balanced diet

9. diagnose me

10. overall health

11. get plenty of sleep

The Goose that Laid the Golden Eggs

Once upon a time in a quaint village, there was a poor farmer named Jack and his wife, Emma. They owned a small farm with a few animals, including a goose. One day, to their surprise, the goose laid a **golden** egg. The couple was overjoyed and couldn't believe their luck.

The news spread quickly, and soon, the whole village learned about the magical goose. Every morning, the goose would lay a single golden egg. Jack and Emma became the talk of the town, and people from far and wide came to witness the extraordinary event.

As time went by, Jack and Emma's life changed. They became more and more **wealthy** with each golden egg, and their once simple farmhouse transformed into a grand **mansion**. The couple was living a comfortable life, thanks to the magical goose.

However, as their wealth grew, so did their **greed**. Jack couldn't help but wonder if there were more golden eggs inside the goose. One day, unable to resist his **curiosity**, he decided to cut the goose open, thinking he could get all the golden eggs at once. To his dismay, the goose had no more golden eggs inside. Jack's hasty decision had cost him the source of his fortune. The couple was left with regret and an ordinary goose.

The moral of the story is that greed can lead to loss. Jack and Emma had a good life with the golden eggs, but their desire for more made them lose everything. It teaches us to be content with what we have and not to let greed cloud our judgment.

And so, the once-magical goose continued to live on the farm, reminding everyone in the village about the consequences of greed. Jack and Emma learned a valuable lesson, and the village returned to its peaceful ways, realizing that true wealth comes from appreciating the blessings we already have.

The Moral

The lesson of the story is: Be happy with what you have and don't be too greedy, or you might lose what's important. With wealth sometimes come **peril.**

Vocabulary

golden: Made of gold.

wealthy: Very rich.

greed: Have a selfish desire for something.

mansion: A very large house.

perils: Serious dangers.

Comprehension Questions

1. What did the special goose do every morning?
2. How did Jack and Emma's life change with the golden eggs?
3. Why did Jack cut open the goose?
4. What happened when Jack cut open the goose?
5. What is the moral of the story?

Answers

1. The special goose laid a golden egg every morning.
2. Jack and Emma became wealthy, and their simple farmhouse turned into a grand mansion.
3. Jack was curious and greedy, thinking there might be more golden eggs inside the goose.
4. To Jack's dismay, there were no more golden eggs, and he lost the magical source of wealth.
5. The moral of the story is to be content with what you have and not let greed lead to losing what's important.

Idioms #7

Pain in the neck

Other forms: A pain in the ass (less polite).

Meaning: Describes someone or something annoying or bothersome.

Origin: From the 1900s, as a more polite way to say, "A pain in the ass."

?Do you know who's a *pain in the neck*? Toby. He keeps asking for junk food before we've even had breakfast."

"I was a *pain in the neck* when I was a teenager. I'm amazed that my parents still love me!"

Play it cool

Meaning: To make an effort to be calm and sensible in a difficult or uncertain situation. It can also refer to dating where you don't want to show someone just how much you like them.

Origin: Unclear.

"Do NOT text her back immediately. You need to *play it cool* and wait for at least a couple of hours."

"I know you want the job but don't you think you should *play it cool* and wait a day or two before following up? I think that'd be better."

Pull yourself together

Meaning: A saying to tell someone to regain their self-control or confidence.

Origin: Uncertain.

"*Pull yourself together* Tammy. You're going to fail math unless you put more time in."

"You need to *pull yourself together*. Your kids need you right now."

Push (someone's) buttons

Meaning: To do something to intentionally make someone angry, upset or frustrated

Origin: From the 1920s, of American origin. Comes from a time when home appliances started requiring just the push of a button to work.

"You're starting to *push my buttons*. I need to take a walk and cool off. Why don't we talk later?"

"You and your brother keep *pushing each other's buttons*. It's time for you guys to go back to school I think."

Rule of thumb

Meaning: General rule about something.

Origin: Various theories:

- Builders who don't measure well and just use an approximate measure (thumb).

- A thumb is generally equivalent to an inch when measuring cloth.

- The thumb is used when brewing beer to gauge temperature.

- An alleged British law that allowed men to beat their wives with sticks no wider than a thumb.

"A good *rule of thumb* is to think about big purchases for at least a week before buying them."

"My *rule of thumb* for keeping my house clean is to always tidy up before I go to bed."

Negotiating with Another Company

Ken and Bob are talking about some negotiations.

Ken: I wanted to **touch base** with you and find out where you're at with that new software we recommend to your company.

Bob: Oh you know Jerry. He likes to **take things slowly** and is reluctant to **shake things up**. What we're currently using is fine for now he thinks. Sorry if I gave you **the wrong impression** that this deal might happen quickly.

Ken: To **go out on a limb** here, if you don't upgrade, you'll likely be **playing catch up** for years **down the road**.

Bob: **Big picture**, we know that. Unfortunately, I don't **call the shots** or **hold the purse strings**. Jerry does.

Vocabulary

touch base: To check in with someone.

take things slowly: To not move quickly.

shake things up: To reorganize something in a drastic or big way.

the wrong impression: To think wrongly about someone, based on a first meeting.

go out on a limb: To take a risk.

playing catch up: To try to reach the same level as others, especially after starting late.

down the road: In the future.

big picture: Considering everything.

call the shots: To make the decisions.

hold the purse strings: To make the financial decisions.

Practice

1. You'll have to talk to Tommy about money stuff. I don't _____.

2. I'm afraid that you've got _____ about our company.

3. Things are fine now but I'm worried about what will happen _____.

4. If we don't upgrade our databases, we'll be _____.

5. I only _____ about HR related things.

6. Can we _____ next week? I'd love to hear how you're doing.

7. My CEO wants to _____ in terms of the kind of people we hire.

8. I don't want to _____ too much here, but someone has to tell you this.

9. I'm a mover and shaker but my boss likes to _____.

10. I know you don't agree with me but I don't think you're looking at the _____.

Answers

1. hold the purse strings

2. the wrong impression

3. down the road

4. playing catch up

5. call the shots

6. touch base

7. shake things up

8. go out on a limb

9. take things slowly

10. big picture

Get Back At

Matt is talking to Harry about how things at work are.

Harry: How are things going at work these days?

Matt: Oh, that's a whole story. Do you remember that coworker of mine, Ted? The one that I don't like? We've been put together on the same team and we **run across** each other multiple times a day now. I could **get by** when I only saw him a couple of times a week but it takes everything in me not to **flip out at** him when I see him on the daily.

Harry: That sounds difficult. Have you **let on** that you don't like him? Maybe he'll just keep his distance?

Matt: I've been trying to send bad vibes his way but he's clueless. One day I'm going to **give in** and **go off on** him. It's inevitable.

Harry: What's the main problem?

Matt: He just keeps talking and won't **get back to** work. His mouth never closes. We're super busy so it's extremely frustrating. I think he spends at least five hours out of the workday just chatting about random things. Everyone is less productive because of him.

Vocabulary

run across: See someone or something randomly, without making a plan to.

get by: Survive.

flip out at: Yell or get angry at someone.

let on: Show your true feeling.

give in: Do something you don't want to do because of pressure of some kind.

go off on: Yell or get angry at someone.

get back to: Return to something you were previously doing.

Practice

1. I've never _____ someone as obnoxious as that guy!

2. Don't _____ and do it for them! The kids have to do their chores.

3. It took everything in me not to _____ my boss.

4. I want to _____ doing yoga every day.

5. Try not to _____ that your brother is annoying you and he'll stop.

6. I think we can _____ with only one car for a while. It'll be way cheaper.

Answers

1. run across

2. give in

3. go off on/flip out at

4. get back to

5. let on

6. get by

Bite the Bullet

Jerry is talking to Linda about buying a car.

Jerry: Hey Linda, so I decided to finally **bite the bullet** and get a new car.

Linda: Oh wow! Did it **break the bank**?

Jerry: Kind of, but I didn't want another **lemon**.

Linda: I know, **when it rains, it pours,** right? Your car was always in the shop!

Jerry: For real. It was so annoying. Now, I just have to **crack the whip** on my employees to get out there and make more money for me to pay for it.

Linda: Don't **discredit** yourself! You're **working your fingers to the bone** too.

Vocabulary

bite the bullet: Doing something that you've been avoiding for a while. For example, someone finally deciding to paint their house after delaying for years.

when it rains, it pours: When more than one bad thing happens at the same time.

crack the whip: To be tough on someone.

break the bank: Something that costs a lot.

a lemon: A reference to a car that needs more repairs than usual.

discredit: Not give someone credit.

working your fingers to the bone: Working very hard, beyond capacity.

Practice

1. I wish he'd just _____ and stop complaining so much!

2. My mom used to _____ and make us all clean the house every Sunday morning.

3. That guy has the worst luck! _____.

4. I hope this new-to-me car I just bought isn't _____.

5. Let's go on a nice vacation but I don't want to _____.

6. I don't want to _____ his success, but his father handed him the job.

7. Take a break Tom! You're _____ lately.

Answers

1. bite the bullet

2. crack the whip

3. When it rain, it pours

4. a lemon

5. break the bank

6. discredit

7. working your fingers to the bone

Art History

Art history, a captivating exploration of humanity's creative endeavors, **unveils** the visual narratives that span the ages. As a discipline that **delves** into the evolution of artistic expressions across different cultures, periods, and styles, art history provides a lens through which we can comprehend the depth and diversity of human imagination. From ancient cave paintings to contemporary installations, art history invites us to **decipher** the meanings, contexts, and techniques that artists employ to communicate their ideas, emotions, and experiences.

The Dawn of Artistic Expression

The journey through art history begins with the earliest forms of creative expression found in prehistoric cave paintings. Dating back tens of thousands of years, these **primitive** artworks, discovered in locations like Lascaux and Altamira, offer a glimpse into the symbolic and ritualistic aspects of early human societies.

The Flourishing of Ancient Civilizations

As civilizations emerged, so did more sophisticated artistic practices. The art of ancient Egypt, with its monumental sculptures and intricate hieroglyphics, reflected a society deeply **intertwined** with religion and the afterlife. Meanwhile, the classical art of ancient Greece celebrated human anatomy and idealized beauty, influencing generations of artists to come.

The Sacred and the Divine in Medieval Art

During the medieval period, art became a powerful tool for conveying religious narratives and spirituality. Illuminated manuscripts, stained glass windows, and religious paintings adorned churches and monasteries, with artists conveying divine themes through symbolic imagery.

The Renaissance: Rebirth of Humanism and Realism

The Renaissance marked a transformative period in art history, characterized by a revival of classical ideas and a renewed focus on humanism. Artists like Leonardo da Vinci and Michelangelo explored the intricacies of human anatomy, perspective, and emotion, ushering in an era of unprecedented realism and innovation.

Baroque: Theatricality and Emotional Intensity

The Baroque period brought forth a dramatic and dynamic style that aimed to evoke strong emotional responses. Artists such as Caravaggio and Rembrandt used chiaroscuro and tenebrism to create intense contrasts of light and shadow, heightening the emotional impact of their works.

Rococo and the Enlightenment

In contrast, the Rococo period embraced a more ornate and decorative aesthetic, reflecting the values of the Enlightenment. Artists like Jean-Honoré Fragonard captured the elegance and refinement of aristocratic life, while others, like Jacques-Louis David, used art as a means to convey political and moral messages.

Romanticism: Nature, Emotion, and the Sublime

The Romantic era celebrated individual expression, emotion, and a deep connection to nature. Artists like J.M.W. Turner and Caspar David Friedrich conveyed the awe-inspiring power of the natural world, exploring themes of the sublime and the transcendent.

Impressionism and Post-Impressionism: Capturing Moments and Emotions

The late 19th century witnessed the emergence of Impressionism, a movement that sought to capture the fleeting effects of light and color. Artists like Claude Monet and Vincent van Gogh challenged traditional techniques, paving the way for Post-Impressionists to explore personal expression and symbolism.

Cubism, Surrealism, and the Avant-Garde

The early 20th century saw the rise of avant-garde movements such as Cubism and Surrealism. Pablo Picasso and Georges Braque deconstructed form in Cubist works, while Salvador Dalí and René Magritte explored the realms of the subconscious and dreams in Surrealist art.

Contemporary Art: Diversity, Conceptualism, and Global Perspectives

The latter half of the 20th century and beyond witnessed a proliferation of artistic styles and mediums. From the abstract expressionism of Jackson Pollock to the conceptual art of Marcel Duchamp, contemporary art reflects a diversity of voices, perspectives, and forms, challenging traditional boundaries and definitions.

Conclusion: Art History as a Window to Cultural Evolution

In conclusion, art history serves as a captivating journey through the visual tapestry of human creativity. From the symbolic imprints of our prehistoric ancestors to the boundary-breaking expressions of contemporary artists, each period reveals the aspirations, values, and societal shifts that shape artistic endeavors. As we explore the vast spectrum of artistic achievements, we gain not only a deeper understanding of the past but also a profound appreciation for the enduring power of artistic expression in shaping our collective human experience.

Vocabulary

art history: The academic discipline that studies the evolution of visual art forms across cultures, periods, and styles, analyzing their cultural, historical, and aesthetic significance.

prehistoric art: Artistic expressions predating written history, often found in the form of cave paintings, carvings, and artifacts, providing insights into early human societies.

renaissance: A period in European art history (14th to 17th centuries) characterized by a revival of classical influences, humanism, and a renewed emphasis on realistic representation.

baroque: An artistic style prevalent in the 17th century known for its dramatic, emotional intensity, ornate detailing, and grandeur in both visual arts and music.

impressionism: An art movement of the late 19th century that focused on capturing the immediate effects of light and color in the natural world, often characterized by loose brushstrokes.

abstract expressionism: A post-World War II art movement emphasizing spontaneous, non-representational forms of expression, often involving large-scale canvases and gestural brushwork.

surrealism: An avant-garde movement of the 20th century that sought to explore the irrational and subconscious realms of the mind, often creating dreamlike and fantastical imagery.

modern art: A broad term encompassing art produced from the late 19th to mid-20th century, marked by a departure from traditional styles and a focus on innovation and experimentation.

contemporary art: Artistic practices from the mid-20th century onwards, reflecting diverse styles, mediums, and themes, often challenging traditional conventions and embracing new technologies.

avant-garde: An experimental and innovative approach to art that pushes the boundaries of established norms, often associated with pioneering movements and artists challenging the status quo.

Vocabulary Challenge

1. Unveils, in the first paragraph is most closely related to:

    a) removes a face or head covering

    b) part of a public ceremony

    c) covers

    d) shows

2. Delves, in the first paragraph is most closely related to:

    a) researches

    b) excavate

    c) reach inside something

    d) dig

3. Decipher, in the first paragraph is most closely related to:

    a) converting one text to another

    b) interpret something

    c) break a code

    d) move water from one place to another

4. Primitive, in the second paragraph is most closely related to:

    a) pre-Renaissance artist

    b) a basic level of comfort

    c) describes something from ancient times

    d) uncomfortable

5. Intertwined, in the third paragraph is most closely related to:

    a) things twisted together

    b) mixed up

    c) mixed into

    d) connected closely

Answers

    1. d

    2. a

    3. c

    4. c

    5. d

Multiple Choice Questions

1. In which historical period did the Renaissance occur?

   a. Ancient Greece

   b. Medieval

   c. Renaissance

   d. Baroque

2. What art movement of the late 19th century focused on capturing the immediate effects of light and color in the natural world?

   a. Baroque

   b. Cubism

   c. Impressionism

   d. Surrealism

3. Which artistic style is characterized by ornate detailing, dramatic intensity, and grandeur, prevalent in the 17th century?

   a. Rococo

   b. Baroque

   c. Renaissance

   d. Neoclassicism

4. What artistic movement emerged in the mid-20th century, emphasizing spontaneous, non-representational forms of expression?

   a. Abstract Expressionism

   b. Cubism

   c. Surrealism

   d. Impressionism

5. Which movement sought to explore the irrational and subconscious realms of the mind, creating dreamlike and fantastical imagery?

a. Cubism

b. Surrealism

c. Impressionism

d. Abstract Expressionism

6. What is the broad term encompassing art produced from the late 19th to mid-20th century, marked by a departure from traditional styles?

a. Renaissance Art

b. Modern Art

c. Baroque Art

d. Impressionist Art

7. Which period preceded the Renaissance and is characterized by art focused on religious themes and symbolism?

a. Ancient Greece

b. Baroque

c. Medieval

d. Rococo

8. What movement challenged traditional conventions and embraced new technologies in art from the mid-20th century onwards?

a. Romanticism

b. Contemporary Art

c. Neoclassicism

d. Abstract Expressionism

9. In which movement did artists like Picasso and Braque deconstruct form and perspective, introducing a fragmented, multi-perspective approach?

a. Surrealism

b. Impressionism

c. Cubism

d. Baroque

10. What term refers to an experimental and innovative approach to art that pushes the boundaries of established norms?

a. Avant-Garde

b. Classicism

c. Renaissance

d. Impressionism

Answers

1. c

2. c

3. b

4. a

5. b

6. b

7. c

8. b

9. c

10. a

Bitter Divorce

Sierra and Brian are talking about their friends getting divorced.

Sierra: Did you **hear the news**? Jeremy and Katie are going through a **bitter divorce**.

Brian: Really? What about the kids? Are they doing **joint custody** or **sole custody**?

Sierra: Joint custody. Jeremy will have them **on weekends** but he has to **pay child support**.

Brian: Poor kids. That was a pretty **dysfunctional family** and they've already had a **troubled childhood**.

Sierra: A **broken home** might be better than all that conflict though. It's too bad that Jeremy and Katie aren't **on good terms**.

Vocabulary

hear the news: Catch the latest gossip.

bitter divorce: A divorce that is hostile with both people feeling angry towards the other.

joint custody: When divorced parents each spend some time taking care of their children.

sole custody: When a divorced parent is responsible 100% of the time for the children.

on weekends: On Saturday and Sunday.

pay child support: When one divorced parent has to give money to the other parent to help pay for the care of the children.

dysfunctional family: A family with many problems.

troubled childhood: Growing up in a family or situation with a lot of problems.

broken home: A home where the parents are divorced.

on good terms: Friendly and get along well.

Practice

1. Thankfully my former boss and I are _____. I need him for a reference.

2. I grew up in a _____ but have worked hard to overcome this.

3. Alex and Jen seem to be doing well with their _____ agreement.

4. Did you _____ ? Jeremy cheated on his wife.

5. _____, I like to spend as much time outside as possible.

6. He's had a _____ so far. I'm surprised that he still does well at school.

7. I want to get _____ of the kids. Tom is a terrible father.

8. I grew up in a _____ and have tried my best to make things better for my kids.

9. I had such a _____ but I'm happy that I don't have to see him anymore.

10. She does _____ but it should be way more than $500 a month I think.

Answers

1. on good terms

2. broken home

3. joint custody

4. hear the news

5. on weekends

6. troubled childhood

7. sole custody

8. dysfunctional family

9. bitter divorce

10. pay child support

The Crow and the Pitcher

Once upon a time, in a sunny meadow bordered by tall trees, there lived a clever crow named Charlie. One scorching summer day, the heat was **unbearable**, and Charlie found himself desperately thirsty. His usual **streams** had dried up, and he began searching for a refreshing drink.

After a relentless search, Charlie finally spotted a **pitcher** partially buried in the ground. Excitement filled him as he hurried towards it, hoping to find some water. However, to his dismay, the water level in the pitcher was too low for him to reach with his beak.

Undeterred, Charlie pondered for a moment. Then, his eyes gleamed with an idea. He looked around and noticed a collection of shiny **pebbles scattered** nearby. With determination, Charlie picked up the pebbles, one by one, and dropped them into the pitcher.

As each pebble fell into the pitcher, the water level gradually rose. Charlie continued this clever strategy, patiently adding more pebbles until the water reached a level where he could finally take a refreshing drink.

His thirst was **quenched**, and Charlie thanked his creativity and problem-solving skills. With a triumphant caw, he flew away, leaving behind a valuable lesson for anyone who witnessed his ingenuity.

The story of Charlie and the pitcher teaches us that intelligence, creativity, and perseverance can help overcome challenges. Instead of giving up when faced with difficulties, like Charlie, we can find innovative solutions by thinking smartly and utilizing the resources around us.

The Moral

The moral of the story is: "Being clever and using your creativity can help you find solutions to problems, even when things seem difficult."

Vocabulary

pitcher: A container used for holding liquids.

pebbles: Small rocks.

streams: Small rivers.

quenched: Satisfied thirst by drinking something.

unbearable: Not able to be endured or tolerated.

scattered: Found in a random fashion, not all together.

Comprehension Questions

1. Why was Charlie the crow thirsty?
2. What did Charlie find when he was thirsty?
3. Why couldn't Charlie reach the water in the pitcher?
4. What did Charlie use to solve the problem and reach the water?
5. What is the moral of the story?

Answers

1. Charlie was thirsty because it was a very hot day, and he couldn't find any water.
2. Charlie found a pitcher with a little water inside.
3. The water in the pitcher was too low for Charlie to reach with his beak.
4. Charlie used shiny pebbles. He dropped them into the pitcher one by one to make the water level rise.
5. The moral of the story is that being clever and using creativity can help find solutions to problems, even when things seem difficult.

Giving Someone the Cold Shoulder

Jerry is talking Linda about his daughter.

Jerry: My daughter called me for the first time **in ages**. She usually **gives me the cold shoulder**.

Linda: Why? What happened to your relationship?

Jerry: Well, we got in a big fight about paying for **grad school.** She was **counting her chickens before they hatch** and assumed I would pay. But, I just didn't have **the dough**. That new car I bought **cost a pretty penny**.

Linda: Yeah, my son only calls **once in a blue moon**. He usually wants some **moola** too! But to be fair, he never misses a Mother's Day card.

Jerry: Kids these days! That seems like the **bare minimum**!

Vocabulary

gives me the cold shoulder: To ignore someone.

once in a blue moon: Rarely.

counting her chickens before they hatch: Counting on something before it's already happened. For example, making plans to go to a certain university before getting the official acceptance letter.

in ages: In a long time.

grad school: Graduate school.

the dough: Money.

moola: Money.

bare minimum: The least someone is obligated to do.

cost a pretty penny: To be expensive.

Practice

1. I wish my kids would do more than the _____ to keep the house clean and tidy.

2. I haven't seen my parents _____ because of Covid.

3. I play tennis _____ because it's always rainy where I live.

4. My neighbour has been _____ lately but I'm not sure why.

5. My daughter is convinced that she'll get into Harvard but I keep telling her to stop _____.

6. I wish that I'd gone to _____ right after I'd finished university.

7. My brother makes the big _____.

8. Give me _____ please!

9. My university education _____. I hope it was worth it!

Answers

1. bare minimum

2. in ages

3. once in a blue moon

4. giving me the cold shoulder

5. counting her chicken before they hatch

6. grad school

7. moola

8. the dough

9. cost a pretty penny

Idioms #8

Sitting on the fence

Meaning: To not come to a conclusion until further information is presented and is convincing enough to make a decision.

Origin: In the middle ages, fences described ownership of property. Someone sitting on the fence describes straddling a position between two properties.

Also has a reference to the Algonquin "Mugquomp" or "important person." It's not a term of respect but instead describes a person not making a decision as a bird on a fence.

"*Sitting on the fence* just isn't going to work here. You're either for this decision, or against it. It's time for you to decide."

"I've been *sitting on the fence* about this because it's a difficult decision. I just don't feel ready to decide."

Take a breather

Meaning: Relax for a while.

Origin: Unknown but likely related to exercise and breathing more heavily than usual.

"Let's *take a breather* for a minute. My brain is tired from working for so long."

"Can I *take a breather,* please? I'm angry right now and need to calm down before we talk about this more."

Take a crack at (something)

Meaning: To attempt an activity that may be uncomfortable or difficult to begin at first.

Origin: Refers to the sound of a crack when a baseball bat hits a ball.

"I'm going to *take a crack at windsurfing*. My daughter loves it and is going to teach me."

"Let's *take a crack at that report* now. I think we have all the information we need."

Take a hike

Meaning: To ask one to go away due to frustration or annoyance.

Origin: Unclear.

"*Take a hike*! She doesn't want to talk to you—she's made that abundantly clear."

"*Take a hike*. I don't want to deal with you right now."

Take a load off

Meaning: To take a break or to help someone out by relieving them of responsibilities.

Origin: From the early 20th century, of American origin. Originally, "take a load off your feet."

"Hey Joe, come sit down for a minute and have a beer. Take a load off."

"Why don't you take a load off and go away for the weekend? You have the weight of the world on your shoulders."

Take a rain check

Meaning: Used in businesses that have something on sale, but not in stock. A customer can ask for a rain check to buy the item at a later date for the sale price. It can also refer to a change of plans, rescheduled at a later date.

Origin: From the late 1800s concerning baseball. It means to postpone a game due to rain where a ticket holder would receive a "rain check" (a ticket to a future game).

"Sorry, I can't come tonight but can I *take a rain check*? I'd love to catch up with you."

"Can I *take a rain check* on that shirt? Do you know when you'll have it back in?"

Bump Into

Jeremy and Owen are talking about someone from high school.

Jeremy: Hey, guess who I **bumped into** today at Starbucks?

Owen: Who?

Jeremy: Tony. Remember him from high school? It **cheered me up** to see him and **catch up**.

Owen: Oh, I see him at the gym all the time and we sometimes even **work out** together. We always say that we need to **get together** but we never **get around to** it.

Jeremy: He seems like a hard guy to **lock down**. He's so busy with his job. Maybe you can **plan ahead** and get a coveted spot on his calendar?

Vocabulary

bumped into: Saw someone unexpectedly.

cheered me up: Made me feel happy.

catch up: Learn what's been happening in someone's life.

work out: Exercise, usually at a gym.

get together: Hang out with each other.

get around to: Deal with or handle something at a future time.

lock down: Make definite plans with someone.

plan ahead: Plan something, not at the last minute.

Practice

1. It's better to _____ for retirement than to be stuck without enough money later.

2. Let's _____ next week and talk about this upcoming project.

3. It _____ to hang out with her new puppy.

4. Guess who I _____ at the grocery store?

5. I want to _____ a definite delivery time.

6. I get grumpy if I can't _____ every day.

7. I'm not sure when I can _____ it. I'll have to check my schedule.

8. Let's grab a coffee and _____.

Answers

1. plan ahead

2. get together

3. cheered me up

4. bumped into

5. lock down

6. work out

7. get around to

8. catch up

Good With Computers

Terry is talking to Sienna about his computer problems.

Terry: Hey, you're **good with computer**s, right? I'm trying to write an essay that's due tomorrow, but my **computer freezes** every couple of minutes. And then . . .

Sienna: Hold on. First things first. Did you **shut down your computer** yet?

Terry: No, should I do that?

Sienna: Yes, and then **restart the computer**.

Terry: Okay, it says it's going to do some **scheduled maintenance** and **install updates**.

Sienna: Let that run and once it starts, do a **virus scan.** It should work a lot better now.

Vocabulary

good with computers: Describes someone who knows how to use computers well.

computer freezes: The computer operating system stops working. For example, you can't click anything on the computer screen

hold on: Wait.

first things first: Do the most important thing first before jumping ahead to other action/things.

shut down your computer: Turn off the computer.

restart the computer: Turn back on the computer after turning it off.

scheduled maintenance: Routine maintenance that helps a computer operating system function well.

install updates: This usually refers to a computer or other electronic device. Involves updating the software.

virus scan: A program that looks for harmful viruses on a computer.

Practice

1. Let's run a _____ first to see if we can catch any problems that way.

2. Just _____ a minute. Did you restart your computer? That's the first thing you should do.

3. Always _____ as soon as possible for your electronic devices to avoid problems.

4. Ted is _____. Let's ask him for some help.

5. _____. Let's get some snacks and drinks for our study session.

6. The network will be down for _____ tonight from 2 am to 4 am.

7. Did you _____ your computer yet? I think that might help.

8. I hate that my _____ at the worst possible times.

9. _____ before going home for the day. I want to save money on electricity.

Answers

1. virus scan
2. hold on
3. install updates
4. good with computers
5. first things first
6. scheduled maintenance
7. restart the computer
8. computer freezes
9. shut down your computer

Unraveling the Tapestry of a Nation

The history of the United States is a rich and complex narrative, weaving together the threads of diverse cultures, social movements, political **upheavals**, and technological advancements. From the Indigenous peoples who first inhabited the continent to the waves of immigrants seeking a new life, American history reflects the continuous **evolution** of a nation marked by **resilience**, innovation, and a quest for freedom.

Early Settlements and Cultures

Long before European colonization, the land now known as the United States was home to a myriad of Indigenous cultures and civilizations. From the Inuit in the Arctic to the Puebloans in the Southwest, these diverse societies developed unique languages, traditions, and ways of life. Native American communities engaged in agriculture, trade, and complex social structures, leaving an **indelible** mark on the continent's history.

Impact of European Colonization

The arrival of European explorers in the late 15th century marked a significant turning point. While explorers like Christopher Columbus sought new trade routes, their presence had profound **consequences** for the Indigenous peoples. The exchange of goods, ideas, and diseases, known as the Columbian Exchange, altered the course of history and set the stage for European colonization.

Establishment of the Thirteen Colonies

The 17th and 18th centuries witnessed the establishment of the Thirteen Colonies along the Atlantic coast. Founded by various European powers, including England, France, and Spain, these colonies became centers of trade, agriculture, and cultural exchange. Each colony developed its own identity, shaped by the ideals of religious freedom, economic opportunity, and self-governance.

Struggles for Independence

Tensions between the American colonies and the British Crown escalated, culminating in the American Revolutionary War (1775-1783). Influential figures like George Washington, Thomas Jefferson, and Benjamin Franklin played pivotal roles in the fight for independence. The Declaration of Independence, adopted in 1776, articulated the ideals of liberty and equality that would shape the emerging nation.

Drafting the Constitution

In 1787, delegates convened in Philadelphia to draft the United States Constitution, laying the foundation for the new republic. The Constitution established the framework of government, balancing power among three branches and incorporating principles of checks and balances. The Bill of Rights, ratified in 1791, enshrined individual freedoms and rights.

Westward Expansion and Manifest Destiny

The 19th century witnessed the westward expansion of the United States, driven by the belief in Manifest Destiny—the idea that Americans were destined to expand across the continent. The acquisition of territories, including the Louisiana Purchase and the Oregon Trail migration, reshaped the nation's geographic and cultural landscape.

Sectional Conflicts and the Civil War

By the mid-19th century, tensions over issues like slavery and states' rights reached a breaking point, leading to the American Civil War (1861-1865). The conflict between the Northern and Southern states tested the nation's commitment to the principles of freedom and equality. The Emancipation Proclamation (1863) and the subsequent abolition of slavery were pivotal moments in shaping the nation's trajectory.

Reconstructing a Nation

The post-Civil War era brought about the challenges of Reconstruction—an attempt to rebuild the South and integrate formerly enslaved individuals into American society. However, the struggle for civil rights and equality persisted, foreshadowing the ongoing battles for justice and equal rights in the years to come.

Industrialization and Progress: The Turn of the 20th Century

The late 19th and early 20th centuries marked a period of rapid industrialization, economic growth, and social change. The Gilded Age, characterized by wealth disparities and political corruption, gave way to the Progressive Era, where reformers sought to address societal issues, improve working conditions, and expand voting rights.

World Wars and Global Influence

The 20th century saw the United States become a global power. The nation played a crucial role in both World War I and World War II, emerging as an economic and military powerhouse. The aftermath of World War II ushered in the Cold War, shaping international relations and influencing domestic policies.

Civil Rights Struggles

The mid-20th century witnessed the Civil Rights Movement—a transformative period in American history. Led by figures like Martin Luther King Jr., Rosa Parks, and Malcolm X, the movement sought to dismantle racial segregation and secure equal rights for African Americans. Landmark legislation, including the Civil Rights Act of 1964 and the Voting Rights Act of 1965, aimed to address systemic injustices.

Challenges and Achievements

The latter half of the 20th century and into the 21st century brought about a series of social, political, and technological changes. From the Vietnam War protests and the counterculture movement to the rise of technology and globalization, the United States navigated a complex landscape of challenges and achievements.

Conclusion: A Tapestry Unfinished

In conclusion, the history of the United States is a dynamic and ongoing narrative that continues to unfold. From the earliest Indigenous civilizations to the complexities of the modern era, the United States has grappled with issues of identity, equality, and justice. As the nation confronts contemporary challenges and embraces its diverse heritage, the tapestry of American history remains a testament to the enduring pursuit of freedom, democracy, and the American Dream.

Vocabulary

indigenous: Referring to the original inhabitants of a place, often used to describe the first peoples who lived in a region before the arrival of settlers or colonizers.

colonization: The process of establishing control over a territory or region by a foreign power, often involving the settlement of people from the colonizing country.

constitution: A written or unwritten set of fundamental principles and laws that establishes the framework for the government and guarantees certain rights to its citizens.

Manifest Destiny: The 19th-century belief that the expansion of the United States across the North American continent was both justified and inevitable, driven by a perceived duty and divine mission.

reconstruction: The period following the American Civil War (1861-1865) during which the United States sought to rebuild the Southern states and integrate former slaves into society.

gilded age: The late 19th-century period characterized by economic growth, industrialization, and wealth accumulation, often contrasted with significant social and political issues.

progressive era: A period in the early 20th century characterized by social and political reform efforts aimed at addressing issues such as corruption, inequality, and labor conditions.

civil rights movement: A series of social and political movements in the mid-20th century advocating for the end of racial segregation, discrimination, and the protection of African American civil rights.

cold war: A geopolitical tension and ideological conflict between the United States and the Soviet Union, lasting from the end of World War II to the collapse of the Soviet Union in 1991.

globalization: The interconnectedness and interdependence of economies, cultures, and societies on a global scale, often facilitated by advancements in technology and communication.

Vocabulary Challenge

1. Upheavals, in the first paragraph is most closely related to:

   a) movements of the Earth's crust

   b) revolutions

   c) changes

   d) changes of leaderships

2. Evolution, in the first paragraph is most closely related to:

   a) a gradual development

   b) how living things change

   c) giving off gas or heat

   d) movement

3. Resilience, in the first paragraph is most closely related to:

   a) toughness

   b) resistance to change

   c) inflexibility

   d) elasticity

4. Indelible, in the second paragraph is most closely related to:

   a) a mark that can't be removed

   b) unable to be eaten

   c) something that can't be forgotten

   d) impressive

5. Consequences, in the third paragraph is most closely related to:

   a) relevance

   b) result of an action

   c) reason

   d) turning point

Answers

1. c

2. a

3. a

4. c

5. b

Multiple Choice Questions

1. Who were the original inhabitants of the land that is now the United States?

   a. European settlers

   b. Indigenous peoples

   c. Asian immigrants

   d. African tribes

2. What term refers to the process of establishing control over a territory by a foreign power?

   a. Expansion

   b. Colonization

   c. Manifest Destiny

   d. Emancipation

3. In which period did the United States seek to rebuild the Southern states and integrate former slaves into society?

   a. Reconstruction

   b. Gilded Age

   c. Progressive Era

   d. Civil War

4. What belief, prevalent in the 19th century, justified the expansion of the United States across North America?

   a. Imperialism

   b. Manifest Destiny

   c. Isolationism

   d. Expansionism

5. Which era was characterized by economic growth, industrialization, and wealth accumulation, alongside social and political challenges?

   a. Reconstruction

   b. Progressive Era

   c. Gilded Age

   d. Cold War

6. What is the term for the period of social and political reform efforts in the early 20th century, addressing issues such as corruption and inequality?

a. Reconstruction

b. Progressive Era

c. Civil Rights Movement

d. Cold War

7. Which movement advocated for the end of racial segregation, discrimination, and the protection of African American civil rights?

a. Women's Suffrage Movement

b. Civil Rights Movement

c. Labor Movement

d. Anti-War Movement

8. What geopolitical tension and ideological conflict existed between the United States and the Soviet Union after World War II?

a. Great Depression

b. Vietnam War

c. Cold War

d. Korean War

9. What term describes the interconnectedness and interdependence of economies, cultures, and societies on a global scale?

a. Isolationism

b. Nationalism

c. Globalization

d. Imperialism

10. In the context of American history, what document established the framework for the government and guaranteed certain rights to its citizens?

    a. Emancipation Proclamation

    b. Bill of Rights

    c. Declaration of Independence

    d. Constitution

Answers

    1. b

    2. b

    3. a

    4. b

    5. c

    6. b

    7. b

    8. c

    9. c

    10. d

Save me a Seat

Jerry and Sid are talking about coming late to class.

Jerry: Hey Sid, can you **save me a seat** in class? I'm going to **come late**.

Sid: **Take your time**. I'll even **take notes** for you. But, why are you always late?

Jerry: You know the cute girls always catch my eye and then I have to stop and talk. But, **keep up the good work** my friend. I love that you always **pay attention** in class.

Sid: Will you ever **evolve** into a responsible student?! Anyway, we should **have lunch** after class. What do you think?

Jerry: Sounds great. **In light of** what a good friend you are, it's **my treat**.

Vocabulary

save me a seat: Hold a chair or spot for someone at an event, meeting, class, etc.

come late: Show up not on time.

take your time: Don't worry about hurrying.

take notes: Write down briefly what is being heard.

keep up the good work: Continue doing the good things you're doing.

pay attention: Look closely; focus.

have lunch: Eat lunch together.

evolve: Develop or improve to a better state; change for the better.

in light of: Taking into consideration.

my treat: I'll pay.

Practice

1. Do you want to _____ next Friday?

2. Please _____! You'll need to know this for your test next week.

3. Our company needs to _____ if we want to survive.

4. If you _____ to Dr. Kim's class, you have to sit in the front row.

5. Jeremy, _____. You did so well on your exam.

6. _____ this new information, we should have another meeting to discuss things.

7. Don't worry about the prices. It's _____.

8. Please _____. I'm going to be a little bit late getting there.

9. Please _____ for this meeting, okay?

10. _____ doing this test. You have two hours to do it. It's more than enough.

Answers

1. have lunch

2. pay attention

3. evolve

4. come late

5. keep up the good work

6. in light of

7. my treat

8. save me a seat

9. take notes

10. take your time

The Clever Woodcutter

In a small village **nestled** between hills and forests, there lived a **woodcutter** named Jack. Jack was known throughout the village for his hard work and honesty. One day, he faced a **dilemma** that would test his cleverness.

One winter morning, as Jack entered the forest to gather firewood, he noticed a large **tree**. Its branches were covered with thick snow, and Jack marveled at it. He decided to chop it down for firewood, but as he swung his axe, something unexpected happened.

The tree, being magical, spoke to Jack. "Dear woodcutter, I am the oldest tree in this forest. **Spare** me, and I will grant you three wishes." Jack, surprised and intrigued, agreed to spare the tree's life. The wise woodcutter thought carefully about his wishes. Instead of asking for wealth or grandeur, Jack chose wisely.

For his first wish, Jack asked for a small, cozy cottage. In an instant, a charming cottage appeared on the edge of the forest. Jack was delighted.

For his second wish, Jack asked for a pouch that would never run out of gold coins. The magical pouch appeared, and every time he reached inside, it was filled with gold. Jack was content but still had one wish left.

For his final wish, Jack thought of the well-being of his village. He asked for the health and prosperity of his fellow villagers. The ancient tree granted his wish, and from that day forward, the village flourished.

Word of Jack's cleverness and kindness spread far and wide. People from neighboring villages came to seek his advice, and Jack became known as the wisest woodcutter in the land.

The Moral

The moral of the story is that true wisdom lies in making choices that benefit not only oneself but also the community. Jack's clever decisions brought prosperity to his village, showing that kindness and selflessness are the keys to a fulfilling life.

Vocabulary

woodcutter: A person who cuts wood.

spare: Save; not use.

nestled: Partially hidden.

dilemma: A problem.

Comprehension Questions

1. What made Jack a wise woodcutter?
2. What did Jack find in the forest one winter day?
3. What did the magical tree offer Jack in exchange for sparing its life?
4. What were Jack's three wishes?
5. How did Jack's choices affect the village?

Answers

1. Jack was considered wise because he made clever choices that not only benefited himself but also brought happiness to his village.
2. Jack found a special, magical tree in the forest.
3. The magical tree offered Jack three wishes in exchange for sparing its life.
4. Jack's first wish was for a cozy cottage, the second wish was for a pouch that never ran out of gold coins, and the third wish was for the health and happiness of his village.
5. Jack's choices brought prosperity and happiness to the village. The health and well-being of the villagers improved, and the village thrived.

Breaking Out in a Cold Sweat

Tom is a mature student who is talking to Jackie about studying for an exam.

Tom: I've been **breaking out in a cold sweat** a lot lately. I'm **a bundle of nerves**. I'm not used to having to study so much.

Jackie: What are you studying for?

Tom: I have to pass this exam for work and I'll lose my job if I don't. I'm maybe **making a mountain of a molehill** but I can't help being nervous about it. It's been so long since I've had to take a test.

Jackie: It's **like riding a bike**. You'll get back into it once you start. **Go with the flow**.

Tom: Do you have any **study tips**?

Jackie: My best advice is to study a little bit every day instead of pulling all-nighters or **cramming**. That doesn't work. Give yourself time to **chew it over**.

Vocabulary

breaking out in a cold sweat: To be afraid or nervous about something.

a bundle of nerves: Describes someone who is very nervous or worried about something.

making a mountain out of a molehill: To make something into a bigger deal than it is. For example, someone who loses sleep over a small problem.

like riding a bike: Something that you always remember how to do, even with a large break in between.

go with the flow: To relax and go along with whatever happens.

study tips: Ideas for how to study more effectively.

cramming: Trying to learn everything for a test at the last minute.

chew it over: In this case, means taking time and not rushing when considering the test material.

Practice

1. You'll get the hang of it. It's _____.

2. This final exam has me _____. I'm so worried about it.

3. I think you need to _____ with this school project. It sounds like you're taking it way more seriously than the other people in your group.

4. I'll have to _____ for a for a few days. Can I let you know next week?

5. I don't think that _____ is a very effective study method.

6. You're _____ right now. Is anything wrong?

7. One of the best _____ is to do it for one hour and then take a 10-minute break.

8. I think you're _____. It's not a big deal!

Answers

1. like riding a bike

2. breaking out in a cold sweat

3. go with the flow

4. chew it over

5. cramming

6. a bundle of nerves

7. study tips

8. making a mountain out of a molehill

Build In

Keith and Jen are talking about their weekend plans.

Keith: Should we talk about our weekend plans?

Jen: Sure, my main priority is **staying up** to watch the Oilers and then **getting up** late the next day. But let's **build in** some time for cleaning and organizing too. Our house is getting so messy.

Keith: I **figured on** that. Let's **pull out** the couch and do a deep clean. And also **put together** that new coffee table. We've been so lazy.

Jen: Let's do it. And what about food? We have that soup from yesterday we can **heat up** for a couple of meals but we'll need to **pick up** groceries.

Keith: Sure thing.

Vocabulary

staying up: Going to bed later than the usual time.

getting up: Waking up.

build in: Allow time for.

figured on: Already knew.

pull out: Take something away from somewhere.

put together: Assemble.

heat up: Make something warm.

pick up: Get something or someone from somewhere.

Practice

1. The kids have been _____ so late during summer vacation.

2. I'll _____ some Thai on my way home from work.

3. I _____ that. I just wanted to check and see if you'd changed your mind.

4. Can you help me _____ my new dresser today?

5. Let's _____ some time to chill out this weekend. We've been so busy these days.

6. _____ early is so difficult for me.

7. Let's _____ the stew for dinner.

8. Let's _____ the bed and vacuum all the dust bunnies.

Answers

1. staying up

2. pick up

3. figured on

4. put together

5. build in

6. getting up

7. heat up

8. pull out

In the Pipeline

A student is commenting on climate change in a class.

I think that all our discussion about climate change **overlooks** one important thing—what we eat. **Cattle** production on **factory farms** releases a massive amount of **methane gas** into the atmosphere, not to mention polluting the local water sources. This is important because it's something that individuals can have an impact on and it's time to **come to grips with** this. We need to eat less meat!

The good news is that there is a shift happening in consumer awareness. More and more plant-based meats are **in the pipeline** and they are becoming increasingly popular with consumers. These new kinds of "meat" have the potential to **transform** the way we eat. I'm **under no illusion** that we'll suddenly have more Vegans because people are worried about climate change. However, plant-based meats **have a lot of potential** if two or three times a week, people choose it instead of beef, pork, or chicken. People would be healthier too!

Vocabulary

overlooks: Fails to notice something.

cattle: A name for cows (more than 1 of them).

factory farms: Large farms that operate on a huge scale.

methane gas: A kind of gas that's released by cows as they digest food.

come to grips with: Begin to deal with.

in the pipeline: something being developed by a person, company, government, etc. that will be available soon.

transform: Dramatic change.

under no illusion: False idea or belief.

have a lot of potential: Has the ability to change into something else in the future.

Practice

1. I'm _____ that this situation will get better.

2. The _____ outside my city pollute the air, land, and water.

3. We have to _____ the fact that climate change is real.

4. _____ is a major contributor to climate change.

5. I want to _____ this piece of land into an organic farm.

6. He _____ but he needs to focus on his studies instead of playing video games.

7. We have a similar product _____. It should be available in about 6 months.

8. I'm so thankful that my teacher _____ so many errors in my writing.

9. I grew up on a farm that raised _____.

Answers

1. under no illusion

2. factory farms

3. come to grips with

4. methane gas

5. transform

6. has a lot of potential

7. in the pipeline

8. overlooks

9. cattle

Crafting Spaces, Shaping Worlds

Architecture, the art and science of designing and constructing structures, is a **profound** expression of human creativity that shapes the environments we inhabit. From towering skyscrapers to humble dwellings, architecture encompasses a spectrum of styles, influences, and functions. This introduction delves into the multifaceted world of architecture, exploring its historical roots, evolving styles, and the impact it has on our daily lives.

Defining Architecture: A Fusion of Art and Science

At its core, architecture is more than just the construction of buildings; it is a **harmonious** blend of art and science, form and function. Architects are not merely builders; they are visionaries who conceive and execute designs that not only serve practical needs but also evoke emotions, tell stories, and reflect cultural identities.

The Architect's Toolkit

Architects employ a diverse toolkit that includes spatial design, structural engineering, environmental considerations, and aesthetic principles. They navigate the complex interplay of materials, light, and space to create structures that stand as **testaments** to human ingenuity and aspiration.

Tracing the Evolution of Architectural Styles

The history of architecture is a tapestry woven with the threads of ancient wonders and classical foundations. From the **majestic** pyramids of Egypt to the timeless beauty of Greek and Roman temples, ancient civilizations laid the groundwork for architectural principles that would endure through the ages.

Medieval Marvels and Gothic Grandeur

In the medieval era, architecture evolved with Gothic grandeur, characterized by soaring cathedrals and **intricate** ornamentation. These structures, often reaching towards the heavens, reflected not only religious devotion but also the technical achievements of the time.

Renaissance Revival and Neoclassical Elegance

The Renaissance witnessed a revival of classical ideals, introducing symmetry, proportion, and perspective into architectural designs. Neoclassical architecture, echoing the grandeur of ancient Greece and Rome, became synonymous with elegance and order.

Modernism to Postmodern Experimentation: 20th Century Paradigms

The 20th century ushered in the era of modernism, emphasizing simplicity, functionality, and the rejection of ornate ornamentation. Pioneers like Le Corbusier and Frank Lloyd Wright embraced the mantra that "form follows function," leading to the creation of sleek, minimalist structures that prioritized utility.

Postmodern Experimentation

As modernism matured, architects embraced postmodernism, breaking free from rigid design principles. Postmodern architecture, characterized by playful experimentation, eclecticism, and a rejection of strict rules, allowed for a more expressive and varied architectural landscape.

Contemporary Trends: Sustainability, Technology, and Beyond

In the 21st century, architecture has become synonymous with sustainability. From green roofs to energy-efficient designs, architects prioritize environmental consciousness, recognizing the crucial role architecture plays in addressing global challenges.

Technological Integration

Advancements in technology have transformed the architectural process. Computer-aided design (CAd), virtual reality simulations, and 3D printing empower architects to visualize and execute designs with unprecedented precision and efficiency.

Inclusive and Responsive Design

`Contemporary architecture also embraces inclusive and responsive design principles. Architects strive to create spaces that cater to diverse needs, promote accessibility, and foster a sense of community.

Architecture in Our Lives: The Power of the Built Environment

Architecture is not confined to blueprints and structures; it profoundly influences the way we live, work, and interact. Thoughtfully designed spaces can enhance community well-being, foster social connections, and contribute to a sense of place and identity.

Aesthetic Pleasures and Emotional Impact

Beyond functionality, architecture offers aesthetic pleasures and emotional impact. A beautifully designed space has the power to evoke joy, inspiration, and a sense of wonder, enriching our daily experiences.

Conclusion: A Constant Evolution

In conclusion, architecture is a dynamic and ever-evolving discipline that reflects the spirit of its time. From ancient wonders to contemporary marvels, architects shape the world we inhabit. As we navigate the diverse landscapes of architectural history and embrace the innovations of the present, we witness the enduring power of architecture to inspire, provoke thought, and enrich the human experience. The built environment, in all its forms, stands as a testament to the endless possibilities when creativity and functionality converge in the pursuit of shaping the world around us.

Vocabulary

architecture: The art and science of designing and constructing buildings or structures, encompassing aesthetic principles, functionality, and the use of materials.

modernism: An architectural movement in the 20th century characterized by a focus on simplicity, functionality, and the rejection of traditional ornamentation in favor of clean lines and minimalism.

postmodernism: A reaction to modernism, postmodernism in architecture embraces eclecticism, experimentation, and a rejection of strict design principles, often incorporating diverse styles and cultural references.

sustainability: In architecture, the concept of creating structures that minimize environmental impact, conserve resources, and promote long-term ecological balance.

urbanism: The study and design of urban spaces, considering factors such as infrastructure, land use, and social dynamics to create functional and aesthetically pleasing environments.

cultural identity: In architecture, the representation and expression of a community's unique cultural characteristics, history, and values in the design of buildings and public spaces.

spatial design: The organization and arrangement of physical spaces to enhance functionality, aesthetics, and user experience, often involving considerations of flow, proportion, and lighting.

inclusive design: An approach in architecture that aims to create environments accessible to all individuals, regardless of physical abilities, promoting inclusivity and diversity.

adaptive reuse: The practice of repurposing existing structures for new uses, preserving historical or architectural significance while meeting contemporary needs.

cadence: In architecture, the rhythmic flow and sequence of spaces within a building, considering the arrangement of rooms and how occupants move through them.

Vocabulary Challenge

1. Profound, in the first paragraph is most closely related to:

    a) very deep

    b) a severe problem

    c) someone with great insight

    d) a great depth

2. Harmonious, in the second paragraph is most closely related to:

   a) a consistent whole

   b) free from dissent

   c) getting along well

   d) in tune

3. Testaments, in the third paragraph is most closely related to:

   a) an old book

   b) a will

   c) found in the Bible

   d) signs of something

4. Majestic, in the fourth paragraph is most closely related to:

   a) related to a queen or king

   b) having beauty

   c) of a great height

   d) royal

5. Intricate, in the fifth paragraph is most closely related to:

   a) Not aesthetically pleasing

   b) having many complex parts

   c) Related to old buildings

   d) too complex to understand

Answers

   1. a

   2. a

   3. d

   4. b

   5. b

Multiple Choice Questions

1. What is the primary goal of sustainable architecture?

    a. Maximizing ornamentation

    b. Minimizing environmental impact

    c. Embracing excessive energy consumption

    d. Prioritizing historical accuracy

2. Which architectural movement emphasizes clean lines, minimalism, and functionality?

    a. Postmodernism

    b. Gothic architecture

    c. Modernism

    d. Neoclassicism

3. What does adaptive reuse in architecture involve?

    a. Constructing entirely new buildings

    b. Repurposing existing structures for new uses

    c. Embracing traditional design principles

    d. Ignoring historical significance

4. In urbanism, what does the term "mixed-use development" refer to?

    a. Exclusive residential areas

    b. Single-purpose commercial spaces

    c. Blending residential and commercial functions in one area

    d. Industrial zones only

5. What characterizes the architectural style of postmodernism?

a. Minimalism and clean lines

b. Eclecticism and experimentation

c. Ornate ornamentation and symmetry

d. Emphasis on historical accuracy

6. What is the purpose of inclusive design in architecture?

a. Exclusivity and elitism

b. Ignoring diverse needs

c. Creating environments accessible to all

d. Focusing solely on aesthetics

7. What does the term "cadence" refer to in architecture?

a. Musical elements incorporated into design

b. Rhythmic flow and sequence of spaces within a building

c. Use of excessive ornamentation

d. Structural engineering principles

8. Which movement rejected strict design principles and embraced cultural references and diverse styles?

a. Neoclassicism

b. Gothic architecture

c. Modernism

d. Postmodernism

9. What is the study and design of cities and urban spaces known as?

a. Architecture

b. Urbanism

c. Sustainability

d. Spatial design

10. In architecture, what does the term "cultural identity" encompass?

a. Representing a community's cultural characteristics in design

b. Ignoring cultural influences in design

c. Focusing solely on functional considerations

d. Rejecting historical significance

Answers

1. b

2. c

3. b

4. c

5. b

6. c

7. b

8. d

9. b

10. a

No Pain No Gain

Jay and Lily are talking about going back to school.

Jay: I'm thinking about going back to school to study engineering! Hitting the books again. Am I crazy? I haven't been in school for years but I'm so tired of my **dead-end job**.

Lily: Well, as I like to say, "**No pain, no gain!**" If you're going to **make some bank** at a new job afterwards, then why not? You can **reinvent** yourself if you want to.

Jay: That's what I thought too. I'm going to enjoy the **calm before the storm** though. I'm going to be **as busy as a beaver** once the semester starts up in September.

Lily: Oh, you'll **weather the storm** just fine and it'll be **happily ever after** for you. You've got a **good head on your shoulders.** Let's get a beer tonight. You can tell me more about your plan.

Vocabulary

dead-end job: A job without possibility of promotion or advancement

no pain, no gain: Stress and difficulties are to be expected when doing hard work for a goal.

make some bank: To earn lots of money.

reinvent: Make something new again.

calm before the storm: A quiet period before a difficult time.

as busy as a beaver: Working a lot or very hard.

weather the storm: Make it through, or survive a difficult situation.

happily ever after: Go through the rest of your life happily.

good head on your shoulders: Has good common sense, good judgement, is practical.

Practice

1. I'm going to work up in northern Canada to _____.

2. I'm just going to enjoy the _____. Things will get crazy with final exams next month.

4. I'm trying to become an engineer. It's tough going but _____.

5. My husband works at a _____. He says the pay is terrible and they don't give raises.

6. You have a _____. You'll be fine at university.

7. Do you think that Tom and Cindy will be a _____ story?

8. It's going to take more than that to _____.

9. I want to _____ myself with a new job that allows for personal growth.

10. He's _____ with that new course he's taking.

Answers

1. make some bank

2. calm before the storm

4. no pain, no gain

5. dead-end job

6. good head on your shoulders

7. happily ever after

8. weather the storm

9. reinvent

10. as busy as a beaver

Idioms #9

Take it with a grain of salt

Meaning: To wearily, or skeptically accept a statement or conclusion.

Origin: To make food more delicious by adding a small amount of salt.

"Honestly, you need to *take whatever she says with a grain of salt*. She's known for exaggerating the truth."

"*Take it with a grain of salt*. You know how she is—always looking on the worst side of things."

Take one for the team

Meaning: To make a sacrifice or accept blame on behalf of a colleague or friend.

Origin: It's possibly a sports reference where it means to sacrifice something for your team.

"You need to *take one for the team* here. Somebody has to stay late and get it done."

"I'm so frustrated that I always have to *take one for the team* just because I don't have kids. It's unfair."

Take someone to the cleaners

Meaning: A gambling reference that means to take all of someone's money or belongings

Origin: Related to the idiom, "clean someone out". First used when laundromats came into existence in the 1920s.

"We can *take him to the cleaners*. He's so naive."

"Let's *take them to the cleaners*. They're so weak and won't be able to fight back against the takeover."

Take stock of (something)

Meaning: To think carefully about something to make a decision; also to remind oneself of previous situations.

Origin: Potentially refers to farmers' belongings. Can also refer to making an itemized list of things.

"Let's *take stock of our situation* before deciding what to do."

"Please *take stock of your financial resources* before deciding to buy a home. Don't forget about things like property taxes, utilities and insurance."

Take (plead) the fifth

Meaning: To refuse to answer a question if the answer may incriminate or embarrass oneself. Instead of answering the question, the person could say, "I plead the fifth."

Origin: Refers to the Fifth Amendment of the United States - "Plead the Fifth." This amendment states that an American citizen cannot be forced to give testimony that could be used against them.

"Whatever you do during the investigation, don't answer any questions about firing that employee. Just *take the fifth* instead."

"I'm so frustrated that that senator keeps *pleading the fifth*. He should have to answer for what he did!"

The third wheel

Meaning: Describes someone who is spending time with a couple. Often that person is unwanted or unnecessary.

Origin: Bicycles have two wheels and cars have four. Three wheels are awkward and unbalanced.

"Let's invite Toby too. I don't want to be *the third wheel* with you and Cindy."

"I hate being *the third wheel.* Tom and Kari invited me to go on vacation but I said no."

The Gnat and the Bull

Once upon a time, there lived a tiny **gnat** named Gerty. Gerty was a curious gnat who loved to explore and make new friends. One day, while **buzzing** around, she saw a big and powerful bull named Benny grazing peacefully in the field.

Gerty decided to strike up a conversation with Benny. "Hello there, Mr. Bull! I'm Gerty. What brings you here?" she asked, buzzing around Benny's **massive** head. Benny, with a friendly grin, replied, "Well, Gerty, I'm here to enjoy the tasty grass and the warm sunshine. What about you? What brings a little gnat like you to this big meadow?"

Gerty giggled, "I love exploring! Do you mind if I hang out with you for a while?" Benny chuckled, "Not at all, Gerty! Feel free to buzz around and keep me company."

As days passed, Gerty and Benny became the best of friends. Gerty would tell Benny stories about her adventures, and Benny would share his experiences of the meadow. They enjoyed each other's company, and their friendship grew stronger. One hot afternoon, a group of other gnats approached Gerty. "Why are you friends with that big, scary bull?" they asked. "He's so much bigger than you!" Gerty smiled and said, "Benny is kind and gentle. Size doesn't matter when it comes to friendship."

The other gnats were skeptical but decided to give it a try. To their surprise, Benny welcomed them with open arms. The gnats soon realized that Benny was not scary. One day, a storm approached the meadow. The other gnats, being so small, **struggled** against the strong winds. Gerty, on the other hand, found refuge on Benny's back.

Benny, with his strength, shielded Gerty and the other gnats from the harsh weather. The gnats, now grateful for their friendship with Benny, huddled together and weathered the storm safely. After the storm passed, the other gnats admitted, "You were right, Gerty. Benny may be big, but he's a true friend."

And so, in the meadow, the gnat and the bull showed everyone that friendship knows no size.

The Moral

The moral of the story is: "Friends can be different sizes, but what matters most is kindness and being there for each other when times get tough."

Vocabulary

gnats: A kind of small fly.

buzzing: Making a low humming sound; moving around.

massive: Huge.

struggled: Had a hard time with.

Comprehension Questions

1. Who is the main character in the story?
2. What is Benny's role in the story?
3. Why do some other gnats doubt Gerty's friendship with Benny?
4. How does Gerty prove that size doesn't matter in friendship?
5. What happens when a storm comes to the meadow?

Answers

1. The main character in the story is a tiny gnat named Gerty.
2. Benny is a big bull and becomes Gerty's friend in the story.
3. They doubt Gerty's friendship with Benny because Benny is much bigger in size.
4. Gerty proves that size doesn't matter by showing kindness and friendship with Benny.
5. Gerty and the other gnats struggle in the storm, but Benny protects them on his back.

Swallow My Pride

Nathan is talking to his friend Zeke about looking for a job.

Zeke: Hey Nathan, how's the **job search** going? Anything going on?

Nathan: Not well. I've been **applying for** jobs but no bites yet. There are so many **job seekers** out there now with the high **unemployment rate**. I might have to **swallow my pride** and take an **entry-level job**. I was hoping for something better but that's not likely now. It's **kind of late in the game**.

Zeke: You could **do an internship**?

Nathan: Nah, I need to **earn money** now. I've got bills to pay with my massive student loans.

Zeke: **Hang in there,** my friend. Any **stable** job isn't a bad thing in this economy.

Vocabulary

job search: The process of looking for a job.

applying for: Seeking employment by sending out applications/resumes/CVs.

job seekers: People who are looking for a job.

unemployment rate: The number of people without jobs measured against the total workforce (listed as a percentage).

swallow my pride: Humble myself.

entry-level job: A job that doesn't require much (or any) experience.

kind of late in the game: Too late in the process to be useful.

do an internship: Work for free to gain experience.

earn money: Make cash.

hang in there: Don't give up.

stable: Secure; not changing.

Practice

1. I want to give up on my _____. I'm not even getting any interviews.

2. _____, okay? I know it's difficult but it'll be worth it when you're done.

3. I had to _____ and apologize to my teacher last week.

4. I'm trying to think of creative ways to _____ this summer.

5. My job isn't _____. I can be laid off at any time.

6. There's a seminar for _____ tomorrow night at the employment center.

7. Sorry, it's not possible. You're _____ for internship applications, aren't you?

8. The _____ is 3.5% in Canada.

9. I think I might _____ to get some experience.

10. Most university graduates take an _____ after they graduate.

11. My goal is _____ at least three jobs a day.

Answers

1. job search

2. hang in there

3. swallow my pride

4. earn money

5. stable

6. job seekers

7. kind of late in the game

8. unemployment rate

9. do an internship

10. entry-level job

11. applying for

Break Up

Tammy is talking to her friend Katrina about her relationship with Tony.

Tammy: I'm thinking about **breaking up** with Tony. We **get along** well but he never **calls me back** and I often feel like he's **brushing me off**.

Katrina: Maybe you're just **growing apart**? At least you don't **live with** him. It'll be easier to break up.

Tammy: Yeah, I kind of wonder if he's **cheating on** me? I always feel like he's **keeping things from** me.

Katrina: Who knows. Anyway, it sounds like you're done. Let's go have some beers and I'll help you **get over** it.

Vocabulary

breaking up: Ending a relationship.

get along: Enjoying each other's company; not fighting.

calls me back: Returns phone calls.

brushing me off: Ignoring; slow to respond to phone calls or text messages.

growing apart: Having less in common than previously.

live with: Sharing a house or apartment with someone.

cheating on: Having sex with another person secretly or without permission.

keeping things from: Not telling someone everything; keeping secrets.

get over: Recover; feel better.

Practice

1. I know it doesn't seem like, but you'll _____ it.

2. My coworker and I _____ so well. We're the dream team!

3. I think she's been _____ her husband with Todd.

4. Maybe you and Tony are just _____. It's not a bad thing. It's natural.

5. _____ wasn't the worst of it. They had to sell their house too.

6. I'm not sure I want to _____ someone. I love my alone time too much.

7. Do you think he's _____? I'm not sure. Maybe he's just busy.

8. I'm wondering if he's _____ me. I just have a weird feeling about it.

9. My son never _____. I'm thinking about making him pay his own phone bill!

Answers

1. get over

2. get along

3. cheating on

4. growing apart

5. breaking up

6. live with

7. brushing me off

8. keeping things from

9. calls me back

Evolution

Lana and Cindy are talking about an article they read about the American education system.

Lana: You wouldn't believe what I read the other day. It was about the **debate** in the USA over what to teach in science classes—**evolution** or **creationism**.

Cindy: I've heard a bit about that. Most other countries **take it for granted** that the **theory** of evolution is a real thing. Not in the USA though. There are many people who **deny** it.

Lana: I know, there's so much evidence for it though. For example, **the fossil record**. Who could deny it? It's not controversial at all!

Cindy: Well, **the driving force** behind it is the Christian Church. They have a lot of **influence** over many spheres of life in the USA, including things like abortion rights.

Lana: I'm not sure why **Joe Public** has so much influence. Scientists should decide what to teach in science class.

Vocabulary

debate: Discussion where people have different viewpoints.

evolution: The theory that humans evolved from earlier forms like apes.

creationism: The theory that God created humans exactly as they are.

take it for granted: Assume that something is true, without questioning it.

theory: A system of ideas to explain something that may, or may not, be true.

deny: Say that something isn't true.

the fossil record: A scientific term. Refers to fossils and the information discovered through them.

the driving force: The power behind something.

influence: Affect someone or something.

Joe Public: The general public's attitude toward a topic (made into a single person).

Practice

1. We can _____ about it all day, but I'm not going to change my mind.

2. You can't _____ that his presentation was excellent, even though you don't like him.

3. Abortion rights. You can't _____ in the USA.

4. How can you not believe in _____? It's clear we descended from apes.

5. You have more _____ with Tony than you think. He always listens to you.

6. In my opinion, evolution isn't a _____. There's so much evidence.

7. I don't care what _____ has to say about it. We need to do the right thing here.

8. The Catholic Church is _____ for many conservative viewpoints in the USA.

9. _____ shows that humans have evolved over millions of years.

10. Many religious people believe in _____.

Answers

1. debate

2. deny

3. take it for granted

4. evolution

5. influence

6. theory

7. Joe Public

8. the driving force

9. the fossil record

10. creationism

The Wolf and the Crane

Once upon a time, in a dense forest, there lived a wolf named Wally. Wally, although strong and fierce, was not the most careful eater. One day, while enjoying a hearty meal, he **accidentally** bit down on a bone, and it got stuck in his throat. Wally tried everything to get the bone out, but it remained lodged, causing him great discomfort. Worried and unable to solve the problem on his own, he decided to seek help.

In the same forest, there was a wise and gentle **crane** named Clara. Clara was known for her long beak, which made her skilled at reaching into tight spots. Wally approached Clara and explained his **predicament**, asking for her assistance.

Clara, being kind-hearted, agreed to help Wally. She gently inserted her long beak into Wally's throat and skillfully maneuvered until she grasped the bone. With a careful and steady pull, Clara successfully removed the bone, relieving Wally from his discomfort. Grateful and humbled by Clara's kindness, Wally apologized for being careless. He realized the importance of being mindful while eating and thanked Clara for her help.

From that day on, Wally and Clara became unlikely friends. Wally learned to eat more carefully, and Clara appreciated the value of helping others in need. Together, they **roamed** the forest, sharing their wisdom and kindness with the other animals.

The story of the wolf and the crane became a lesson for all the **creatures** in the forest — a reminder that kindness and cooperation could overcome even the trickiest of situations. And so, the forest thrived with newfound friendships and a sense of unity, all thanks to the unlikely alliance between a wolf and a crane.

The Moral

The moral of the story is: "It's important to help each other, even if we are different. Working together makes things better for everyone."

Vocabulary

accidentally: Not on purpose.

crane: A kind of bird with a long neck.

predicament: A difficult or unpleasant situation.

roamed: Moved around freely.

creatures: An animal (not a human).

Comprehension Questions

1. Why did Wally, the wolf, need help?
2. Who helped Wally, and what was special about her?
3. What did Clara do to help Wally?
4. How did Wally feel after Clara helped him?
5. What did Wally learn from the experience?

Answers

1. Wally needed help because he accidentally got a bone stuck in his throat.
2. Clara, the crane, helped Wally. She had a long beak that was helpful in reaching into tight spots.
3. Clara used her long beak to carefully take out the bone from Wally's throat.
4. Wally felt relieved and thankful after Clara helped him.
5. Wally learned to be more careful while eating to avoid such problems in the future.

Wrap Up

Tommy and is coworkers are finishing up for the day.

Tommy: Okay, let's **wrap up** and **get out** of here. Joe, can you **turn off** all the lights? Kim, please make sure everyone is **logged off** the network and **shut down** all the computers.

Carrie: I don't want to just **stand around**. What should I do?

Tommy: Oh, why don't you **put away** all the dishes in the lunchroom? And then **switch off** the lights in there when you're done.

Carrie: **Watch out** weekend! Here we come.

Vocabulary

wrap up: Finish.

get out: Leave.

turn off: Stop something from working.

logged off: When you sign out of your account on an electronic device.

shut down: Close or stop something.

stand around: Someone not doing any work does this.

put away: Make sure everything is in its' proper place.

switch off: Stop something from working.

watch out: Look for something; be alert.

Practice

1. Oh _____. The ball is coming right towards us.

2. Were you _____ that account before you left last night?

3. Don't forget to _____ the lights before leaving for work.

4. If you're just going to _____, you could at least hold my tools for me.

5. Let's _____ all the appliances before going on vacation.

6. Did you _____ yet? I'm hoping we can have dinner together tonight.

7. We'll have to _____ the network. We need to do some database maintenance.

8. Please _____ all your toys before bedtime.

9. I'm hoping to _____ for a hike this weekend.

Answers

1. watch out

2. logged off

3. turn off

4. stand around

5. switch off

6. wrap up

7. shut down

8. put away

9. get out

Weather Forecast

Ted and Lindsay are looking at the weather forecast and making plans for the weekend.

Ted: What's the **weather forecast** looking like this weekend? We should get out for a hike.

Lindsay: Let me check. Clear skies on Saturday but **scattered showers** on Sunday. **Hot and humid** both days.

Ted: If we're going to go to Mount Hood, we need to be **prepared for anything**. It can go from calm to **gale-force winds on a dime**.

Lindsay: That happened last time I was there. Just **light rain** at first and then the **storm clouds** rolled in and there were **wind gusts** of more than 100 km/h. It was wild.

Vocabulary

weather forecast: Prediction of future weather.

let me check: Give me a minute to find the answer to something.

clear skies: Not cloudy.

scattered showers: Rain that is on and off.

hot and humid: Muggy.

prepared for anything: Ready to face any situation.

gale-force winds: Very strong wind.

on a dime: Suddenly.

light rain: Not raining heavily.

storm clouds: Clouds that may produce rain, snow, hail, thunder, etc.

wind gusts: Bursts of wind after periods of relative calm.

Practice

1. There will be _____ of more than 150 km/hour today.

2. _____ at night usually means good weather the next day.

3. His personality changes _____.

4. It's so _____. I just want to sit next to a pool.

5. You have to be _____ with this job.

6. I'm not sure if we have that in stock. _____.

7. There are some serious _____ over there. I think we should turn around.

8. The forecast showed some _____. Don't forget your umbrella.

9. What's the _____ for Japan this week? I need to know how to pack for my trip.

10. I know it doesn't seem like it, but _____ are not ideal when sailing.

Answers

1. wind gusts

2. clear skies

3. on a dime

4. hot and humid

5. prepared for anything

6. let me check

7. storm clouds

8. scattered showers/light rain

9. weather forecast

10. gale-force winds

The Fox and the Hedgehog

Once upon a time, in a quiet meadow, there lived a clever fox named Felix and a wise **hedgehog** named Hazel. Felix was known for his sly tricks, and Hazel was known for her sharp mind.

One sunny day, Felix strolled through the meadow, looking for a snack. Spotting Hazel curled up in a cozy corner, he decided to have a little fun. "Hello, Hazel! I heard you know everything. Is that true?" Felix teased.

Hazel, not easily **fooled**, replied, "I know a thing or two. What brings you here, Felix?" Felix, with a mischievous grin, said, "I've heard you can predict the weather. Is that right?"

Hazel chuckled, "Well, not exactly. But I can feel changes in the air and tell when it might rain or when the sun will shine." Felix, trying to be clever, challenged Hazel, "I bet you can't tell me what I had for breakfast this morning!"

Hazel, staying calm, said, "Ah, that's a different skill. I can't do that, but I can tell you're a smart fox who enjoys a good meal." Felix, realizing he couldn't **outsmart** Hazel, decided to change his approach. "Hazel, I'm curious. Why do you always curl up in a ball?"

Hazel smiled, "It's my way of staying safe. When I curl up, my spiky **quills** protect me from potential dangers." Felix, impressed by Hazel's wisdom, admitted, "You may not fall for my **tricks**, but I can see you're a smart hedgehog. Can we be friends?"

Hazel gladly agreed, and from that day on, Felix and Hazel became unlikely but wonderful friends. Felix learned that not everything could be outsmarted, and sometimes, it was better to appreciate the unique qualities of others.

The meadow echoed with the laughter and chatter of the fox and the hedgehog, teaching all the animals that even those with different skills and personalities could find common ground and build lasting friendships.

The Moral

The moral of the story is: "It's nice to be friends with people who are different from us. We can learn from each other and have fun together."

Vocabulary

hedgehog: A kind of animal.

tricks: Things intended to outsmart or outwit someone.

outsmart: Get the better of someone by using the mind.

fooled: Tricked.

quills: The hollow, sharp spines of a hedgehog (and other animals too).

Comprehension Questions

1. Who are the two main characters in the story?
2. What was Felix known for?
3. How did Hazel protect herself from potential dangers?
4. Why did Felix want to be friends with Hazel?
5. What did the other animals in the meadow learn from Felix and Hazel's friendship?

Answers

1. The two main characters in the story are Felix, the clever fox, and Hazel, the wise hedgehog.
2. Felix was known for his clever tricks.
3. Hazel protected herself by curling up in a ball, using her spiky quills.
4. Felix wanted to be friends with Hazel because he realized she was smart and couldn't be easily tricked.
5. The other animals learned that different friends could get along and have fun together.

From Dawn Till Dusk

Eric is asking Mandy how work is going.

Eric: How's work going **these days**?

Mandy: Same old, same old. I have to work **from dawn till dusk**. We have all these **strict deadlines** from clients and are always **running out of time**.

Eric: Can you **cut back on** your hours? That's terrible not having any **free time**.

Mandy: Not if I want to **get ahead** in this industry. I'd love to **take my time** on projects and not be **in a rush** too. But, that's **not going to cut it**.

Vocabulary

these days: Lately.

same old, same old: Nothing has changed.

from dawn till dusk: Working very long hours (early morning to late at night).

strict deadlines: A definite time when something needs to be finished.

running out of time: Lacking time to finish or do something.

cut back on: Reduce.

free time: Leisure time when not working or studying.

get ahead: Make gains, especially compared to other people.

take my time: Not hurry.

in a rush: The need to do something quickly.

not going to cut it: Something you do isn't good enough.

Practice

1. Please do it again. That's _____.

2. I hate having to work under _____. It's very stressful.

3. In my _____, I love to hang out with friends.

4. He's always _____ with his math homework and gets so many answers wrong.

5. I have to work _____ during the year-end.

6. I'd love to _____ my drinking but it's difficult around the holidays.

7. Covid-19 has impacted my social life! It's _____ around here.

8. I'd love to _____ and make a good decision about which program to take.

9. It's difficult to _____ in Vancouver when housing is so expensive.

10. _____, I'm trying to get in better shape.

11. We're _____ and will need to stay late tonight.

Answers

1. not going to cut it

2. strict deadlines

3. free time

4. in a rush

5. from dawn till dusk

6. cut back on

7. same old, same old

8. take my time

9. get ahead

10. these days

11. running out of time

Fell Off

Kent is talking to Gary about his drinking.

Gary: Hey, how's your no-drinking November going?

Kent: Oh, not good. I **fell off** the wagon last weekend and **went out** with my friends. Alcohol is so difficult for me to **give up**.

Gary: Well, get back on the wagon. It's not too late to **start over.** And why don't you **come on** a hike with me this weekend? We can do something healthy.

Kent: I'd love to **take you up on** that and **try out** something new.

Gary: Perfect! I'll **get in touch** with you later this week about the details.

Vocabulary

fell off: Come off of something (a bike, skateboard, etc.)

went out: Left the house.

give up: Stop trying.

start over: Begin again.

come on: Join together.

take you up on: Agree to an offer.

try out: Experiment with something new.

get in touch: Call, text, email, etc.

Practice

1. I _____ my bike and broke my wrist.

2. Are you serious about driving me to the airport? I may _____ that.

3. I want to _____ potato chips but they're so delicious.

4. I want to _____ that trip but it's kind of expensive for me.

5. There's no other option but to _____ with this.

6. Let's _____ that new Italian place tonight.

7. Okay. He finally _____. Let's see if we can break into his computer.

8. Please _____ with Carrie. She's left a few messages now.

Answers

1. fell off

2. take you up on

3. give up

4. come on

5. start over

6. try out

7. went out

8. get in touch

Emotional Wreck

Nathan is telling Jeremy about his weekend.

Jeremy: Hey, how was your weekend?

Nathan: It started well. I **went swimming** with the kids and **did yoga**. But, Tim **broke his leg** at his **soccer game**. He has a **vivid imagination** so I didn't believe him at first but we **went to the hospital** and there was a big break. I'm an **emotional wreck** right now.

Jeremy: Oh, that sounds like tough times. I hope he's okay.

Nathan: He'll recover but he has to have a cast on for at least six weeks. What did you get up to?

Jeremy: I **played tennis** and had a **first date** with someone I **met online.** It went well and we're going to see each other next weekend.

Vocabulary

went swimming: Swam.

did yoga: Did a yoga workout.

broke his leg: Broke a bone in his leg.

soccer game: A soccer match.

vivid imagination: Active imagination.

emotional wreck: In a bad state; anxious, worried, depressed, etc.

played tennis: Had a tennis game or practice.

first date: Spending time together with a romantic interest for the first time.

met online: Meeting a romantic partner on a dating app like *Tinder* as opposed to in real life.

Practice

1. My husband and I _____.

2. My daughter has a _____.

3. I _____ this morning and now I feel great. I'm so relaxed!

4. I had a _____ with someone last night and I think we're going to meet up again.

5. I _____ with my kids but it was frustrating because they couldn't hit the ball well.

6. I _____ this morning very early. I got there when the pool opened at 6:00.

7. Will you come to watch my _____ this weekend?

8. I was an _____ when my grandmother died.

9. My husband _____ at work last week and will be off for at least three months.

Answers

1. met online

2. vivid imagination

3. did yoga

4. first date

5. played tennis

6. went swimming

7. soccer game

8. emotional wreck

9. broke his leg

The Frog who Desired to be a King

Once upon a time, in a peaceful pond, lived a frog named Freddy. Freddy wasn't just an ordinary frog; he dreamt of being a king. He often spent his days imagining what it would be like to rule the pond and have all the other creatures respect and admire him.

One day, as Freddy was croaking by the water lilies, a wise old turtle named Tessa approached him. Tessa had seen many seasons come and go and had witnessed the dreams of many pond **inhabitants**.

"Freddy, my young friend, why do you desire to be a king?" Tessa inquired, her voice slow and gentle. Freddy puffed up his chest and replied, "I want to be respected and admired by everyone in the pond. I want to be the king!"

Tessa, with a knowing smile, **cautioned** Freddy, "Being a king is not just about admiration; it comes with responsibilities and challenges. Are you sure you understand what it means?" But Freddy was too enchanted by the idea of being a king to listen. He hopped around the pond, declaring himself the future ruler.

Word spread quickly, and the other pond creatures were curious. They gathered around Freddy, expecting him to demonstrate his kingly qualities. Freddy, trying to act regal, ordered the fish to bring him the juiciest insects, and the dragonflies to fan him with their wings. However, he found out that being a king required more than just giving orders and being **bossy**.

The pond animals soon grew tired of Freddy's **demanding** behavior. The dragonflies stopped fanning, and the fish swam away in frustration. Feeling lonely and realizing that being a king wasn't as glamorous as he thought, Freddy approached Tessa with a humbled spirit. "Tessa, I now understand that being a king is about more than just being admired. It's about taking care of others and being responsible."

Tessa nodded in agreement, "True leadership comes from humility, responsibility, and care for others. Remember, respect is earned through actions, not just titles." From that day forward, Freddy embraced his role as a responsible and caring member of the pond community. He may not have been a king, but he was respected for his kindness.

The Moral

The moral of the story is: "Being respected is not just about having a big title; it comes from being responsible, kind, and caring for others."

Vocabulary

bossy: Describes someone who likes to tell others what to do.

demanding: Someone who expects a lot of others.

inhabitants: Creatures or people who live in a place.

cautioned: Warned.

Comprehension Questions

1. What did Freddy, the frog, dream of becoming?
2. Who warned Freddy about the responsibilities of being a king?
3. What happened when Freddy tried to act like a king?
4. What did Freddy realize after the other animals stopped listening to him?
5. How did Freddy earn respect in the end?

Answers

1. Freddy dreamed of becoming the king of the pond.
2. Tessa, the old turtle, warned Freddy about the responsibilities of being a king.
3. The other pond animals grew tired of Freddy's bossy behavior and stopped doing what he asked.
4. Freddy realized that being a king wasn't just about giving orders; it involved more responsibilities and kindness.
5. Freddy earned respect by being a kind and responsible member of the pond, even though he wasn't a king.

Eating Habits

Sun and Todd are talking about New Year's resolutions.

Sun: Do you have a **New Year's resolution** planned for 2021?

Todd: A big one! I want to change my **eating habits** by not eating so much **junk food** and **processed food**. I'm going to focus on **home-cooked meals** and smaller **portion sizes**.

Sun: Mine is very similar. I'm not going to **go on a diet** but I want to eat a **balanced diet** with more **fruits and vegetables**. And I want to avoid the **second helpings**, especially at dinner. That's my **Achilles heel**.

Todd: We should **hold each other accountable**.

Sun: Great idea!

Vocabulary

New Year's resolution: Thing you resolve to do for the upcoming year.

eating habits: General way of eating (can be healthy or unhealthy).

junk food: Food that isn't healthy. For example, chips and candy.

processed food: Food that has been manufactured in some way. Often contains lots of sugar, fat and salt.

home-cooked meals: Food that you cook at home.

portion sizes: How much food you eat at one time.

go on a diet: Eat less or differently to try to lose weight.

balanced diet: A wide variety of healthy foods.

fruits and vegetables: Fruits and vegetables!

second helpings: Taking a second portion of a meal after finishing your first portion.

Achilles heel: A weakness in someone who is generally strong.

hold each other accountable: Check in with each other to help achieve some goal.

Practice

1. Let's _____ for this. I want to get this done under budget.

2. My son eats way too much _____. He probably eats an entire box of crackers a day!

3. I want to _____ so that I can lose weight for my sister's wedding.

4. His _____ is that he procrastinates.

5. Avoid _____ at dinner if you want to drop a few pounds.

6. I love _____ like potato chips and candy.

7. I want to reduce my _____. For example, only one piece of chicken instead of two.

8. It's best to eat a variety of brightly colored _____.

9. My _____are terrible. I often skip breakfast and then snack late at night.

10. I love my husband's _____.

11. My _____ is to stop smoking.

12. A _____ consists of healthy foods from a variety of food groups.

Answers

1. hold each other accountable

2. processed food

3. go on a diet

4. Achilles heel

5. second helpings

6. junk food

7. portion sizes

8. fruits and vegetables

9. eating habits

10. home-cooked meals

11. New Year's resolution

12. balanced diet

Give Out

Craig is talking to Tina about grading essays.

Tina: Hey, how's your grading going?

Craig: Uggghhhh. Terrible. I hate grading essays. My university requires that I **mark down** every single little mistake and prove why I gave every grade that I did. It **takes up** so much time.

Tina: Why not **give out** an A to everyone?

Craig: I have to **grade on a curve**. I wish I could do that! I'd be the most popular professor. Honestly though. I dread **handing back** the papers. So many people are unhappy with me.

Tina: Could you **put up** the grades online and not **deal with** it?

Craig: Unfortunately, no. The point is that the students can see their mistakes and **learn from** them. It's not ideal but it's what I have to do.

Vocabulary

mark down: Write.

takes up: Uses; requires.

give out: Distribute something.

grade on a curve: Assign marks according to a certain percentage of A/B/C, etc.

handing back: Returning something.

put up: Post.

deal with: Handle.

learn from: Gain knowledge from something.

Practice

1. Please _____ the changes that you make. I want to know what you did.

2. I don't want to _____ this right now. Can we talk about it later?

3. My new puppy _____ all my free time these days.

4. Will you help me _____ my pictures this weekend?

5. I find it quite difficult to _____.

6. It's okay to make mistakes but the key is to _____ them.

7. Let's _____ full-size chocolate bars for Halloween this year! We'll be so popular.

8. Teachers must hate _____ tests. There are always disappointed students.

Answers

1. mark down

2. deal with

3. takes up

4. put up

5. grade on a curve

6. learn from

7. give out

8. handing back

Business Trip

Jill is talking to Cayla about her trip.

Cayla: How was your **business trip**?

Jill: It was a nightmare. We were packed in like sardines. It was a **bumpy flight** with lots of **crying babies**. There was barely any room for my **carry-on luggage**. We **took off late** and I had to run to catch my **connecting flight**. To top it all off, my **checked luggage** arrived one day late.

Cayla: Wow! That's too much. I'm **amazed by** your bad luck.

Jill: I know, right? I shouldn't complain though. At least it's my **dream job** and I only have to travel **once in a while**.

Vocabulary

business trip: Travel for work.

bumpy flight: Turbulence while flying.

crying babies: Often refers to young children making lots of noise on a plane, bus, etc.

carry-on-luggage: Bags that you store in the plane under your seat or above you.

took off late: Describes a plane that departed after the scheduled time.

connecting flight: An intermediate flight between departing city and destination.

checked luggage: Bags that you give the ticket agent at the airport which are inaccessible while flying.

amazed by: Impressed with.

dream job: An ideal job.

once in a while: Not that often.

Practice

1. Tennis isn't my favourite sport but I'll play with my wife _____.

2. We _____ because someone wouldn't put their seat belt on.

3. My _____ is to be a doctor.

4. The _____ arrived late which meant I was late getting to my meeting.

5. I need to go on a _____ next week to meet with our new clients.

6. I only take _____ when I travel because I hate waiting for my bags after a flight.

7. I'm _____ how well you did on that exam.

8. Thankfully, there were no _____ on my flight.

9. It's usually a _____ from Edmonton to Vancouver.

10. You can find your _____ at carousel four.

Answers

1. once in a while

2. took off late

3. dream job

4. connecting flight

5. business trip

6. carry-on luggage

7. amazed by

8. crying babies

9. bumpy flight

10. checked luggage

The Lion and the Mouse

In a vast savannah, there lived a mighty lion named Leo and a tiny mouse named Molly. Leo was known as the king of the jungle, and Molly was a small creature **scurrying** about the grass, always careful not to disturb the larger animals.

One day, Leo was taking a nap under a shady tree when Molly **accidentally** woke him up. Startled, Leo roared, and Molly **trembled** with fear. Expecting the lion to devour her, Molly apologized, "I'm so sorry, Leo! I didn't mean to disturb you." Leo, amused by the little mouse, decided to show mercy. He smiled and said, "I'll let you go, Molly. Just be more careful next time."

Grateful for Leo's kindness, Molly promised, "Thank you, Leo! I'll remember this, and one day, I might be able to help you too." Leo chuckled at the thought of needing help from such a small creature but let Molly go on her way.

Days passed, and one afternoon, Leo found himself trapped in a **hunter**'s net. Roaring for help attracted the attention of nearby animals, but they were afraid to approach the mighty lion. Just as Leo was losing hope, he felt a tickling sensation on his paw. It was Molly, the tiny mouse, **chewing** through the net with her sharp teeth.

In no time, Molly set Leo free, and the mighty lion was humbled by the small mouse's bravery and kindness. Leo thanked Molly sincerely, realizing that help can come from the most unexpected places.

From that day on, Leo and Molly became unlikely friends, teaching all the animals in the savannah that size and strength don't determine the value of a friendship. And so, the story of the lion and the mouse became a tale of **gratitude**, kindness, and the importance of helping one another, no matter how big or small.

The Moral

The moral of the story is: "Kindness is important, and friends can help each other no matter how big or small they are."

Vocabulary

accidentally: Not on purpose.

chewed: Used teeth to bite something, usually food.

hunter: Someone who kills animals for food or sport.

gratitude: Thankfulness.

scurrying: Moved very quickly.

trembled: Shook.

Comprehension Questions

1. Who are the two main characters in the story?
2. What does Leo, the lion, decide to do when Molly accidentally wakes him up?
3. What does Molly promise Leo after he shows kindness?
4. How does Molly help Leo when he gets stuck in a net?
5. What does Leo learn from Molly's help?

Answers

1. The two main characters in the story are Leo, the lion, and Molly, the mouse.
2. Instead of getting angry, Leo decides to let Molly go, asking her to be more careful.
3. Molly promises to help Leo someday.
4. Molly uses her sharp teeth to chew through the net and set Leo free.
5. Leo learns that friends can be found in unexpected places, no matter their size.

Sitting on the Fence

Toby is talking to Ken about where he's doing to do his Ph.D.

Ken: Have you decided where you want to do your **Ph.D.** yet?

Toby: I'm **sitting on the fence** for now! I haven't chosen a **specific** professor or university. But I do think that I want to be an **international student** so I'm considering Europe.

Ken: Oh, how exciting! Which country?

Toby: I'm not sure yet. I'm applying for some **scholarships**. I don't want to live in poverty. It **boils down to** housing. I want a place that has **dormitory** options for **mature students**.

Ken: Well, I'm sure you'll **figure it out**. Any **university** would be lucky to have you

Vocabulary

Ph.D.: Highest academic degree. Often necessary to become a professor at a university or college. A master's is a 1–2 year program that can prepare you for a career. A PhD, or doctoral degree, takes 3–7 years and prepares you for a career in academic research.

sitting on the fence: Not deciding about something.

specific: A certain thing, preference, etc.

international student: Someone who goes to school in another country.

scholarships: Free money that covers a part of or all tuition (and sometimes books/housing).

boils down to: Refers to the most important thing or aspect of a situation.

dormitory: A place where students live, usually on campus.

mature students: Refers to a student who is older than other students in a year or program.

figure it out: Decide on something.

University: Usually an educational institute that offers 4 year undergraduate degrees, master's degree programs, and Ph.D. programs. Also known as "college" in some countries (for example, the USA).

Practice

1. Only a few people are planning to do a _____ when we're done with this program.

2. I'm applying for lots of _____ but I haven't heard back yet.

3. Is there a _____ reason why I got a C on this paper? I'd like to improve for the next one.

4. Which _____ did you go to?

5. I'm _____ about which program to take. Both options seem good.

6. There are many _____ in my program.

7. I lived in the _____ my first two years of college.

8. Let me take a look at the numbers and see if I can _____.

9. I'm not sure which job I'll take but it will probably _____ salary.

10. An _____ at UBC has to pay $50,000 a year in tuition. It's so expensive!

Answers

1. Ph.D.

2. scholarships

3. specific

4. university

5. sitting on the fence

6. mature students

7. dormitory

8. figure it out

9. boil down to

10. international student

Holding Up

Andy is talking to his girlfriend about a problem at their house.

Andy: Hey Nicole. The drain is **clogged up** again with your long hairs. You're not **holding up** your end of the bargain. Remember? You promised to clean the sink and I promised to **knock off** the late-night video gaming.

Nicole: Oh, **come off it**. It's not a big deal. I could **do with** you not hassling me all the time.

Andy: You **went back on** your word! I **carried out** my end of the deal. You **let me down**.

Nicole: Okay, you're right. I **messed up** and I'm sorry. I'll pay more attention to it.

Vocabulary

clogged up: Blocked.

holding up: Doing something you promised.

knock off: Stop.

come off it: Stop saying something silly or ridiculous.

do with: Get something you want.

went back on: Didn't follow through; broke a promise.

carried out: Did something as promised.

let me down: Disappointed me.

messed up: Did something incorrectly.

Practice

1. Sorry. I _____ on that project. I'll do my best to fix it.

2. He _____ his word—I was so disappointed in him.

3. He's famous for not _____ his end of the deal. Such a sketchy guy.

4. I have a feeling he's going to _____ in the end but so far, so good.

5. I could _____ a cup of tea.

6. The drain is _____ again. Could you please take a look at it?

7. He _____ each task efficiently and under budget.

8. Oh, _____. That's not what happened.

9. Please _____ all the swearing around Jamie, okay? I don't want her to hear that stuff at home.

Answers

1. messed up

2. went back on

3. holding up

4. let me down

5. do with

6. clogged up

7. carried out

8. come off it

9. knock off

Opening Night

Sid and Manny are talking about the new James Bond movie.

Sid: Are you going to watch that new James Bond movie? It **comes out** on the 22nd.

Manny: Oh yeah, I never miss an **opening night** for a Bond movie. I've seen the **movie trailer** at least 10 times now. It's going to be a huge **box office hit**.

Sid: I heard that Tom Cruise has a **supporting role** and that Brad Pitt plays the **main character**. That's pretty impressive.

Manny: For sure. What about you? Will you be there on opening night?

Sid: Not in the **movie theater** but I'll watch it when I can **download it for free**!

Vocabulary

comes out: Begins.

opening night: The first night of something (movie, play, etc.)

movie trailer: A short teaser to entice you to watch the full movie.

box office hit: A movie that makes lots of money.

supporting role: Not the lead actor/actress.

main character: The leading person in a book/movie/TV show, etc.

movie theater: Place you watch movies.

download it for free: Getting a movie/TV show/software/music from the Internet and not paying for it.

Practice

1. Why pay for it when you can _____?

2. Do you know when that _____ on Netflix?

3. Do you think our local _____ will survive Covid-19?

4. Have you seen the _____ for that one yet?

5. The _____ in that book was so complex.

6. She was amazing in that _____. She stole the show.

7. I love to go to a play's _____. There's a different kind of buzz.

8. What's going to be the _____ of the year?

Answers

1. download it for free

2. comes out

3. movie theater

4. movie trailer

5. main character

6. supporting role

7. opening night

8. box office hit

Idioms #10

Through thick and thin

Meaning: To commit to something or someone despite any difficult challenges that may arise over time.

Origin: Dates to the 1300s. It describes a forest where some areas are densely grown, whereas other areas are easy to navigate because they aren't as dense.

"My wife and I have been together *through thick and thin*."

"I don't understand why you're sticking with that company *through thick and thin.* They have never paid you enough for what you do."

Throw (someone) for a loop

Meaning: To be confused or disoriented by an event or statement.

Origin: This could refer to a boxing match in which a person is struck in the head and becomes disoriented.

"She *threw me for a loop* when she fired Nancy. I know she wasn't great but she also wasn't terrible."

"My husband was *thrown for a loop* when he found out that he had cancer. He's so young and healthy that it was a big surprise."

Time is money

Meaning: Refers to the valuable, sometimes monetary nature of time.

Origin: First used by Benjamin Franklin (founding father of the USA) in 1748.

"Let's get back to work. *Time is money!*"

"I need to run. *Time is money* and I have a lot to do."

To make a long story short

Meaning: An expression that is used to explain something in just a few words, instead of giving the entire story.

Origin: A similar saying was first seen in a letter by Henry David Thoreau in 1857.

"*To make a long story short*, I ended up flunking out of medical school."

"It's getting late! *To make a long story short,* I ended up breaking up with Ted and getting together with Chris."

To make matters worse

Meaning: To make an already bad situation even more so.

Origin: Uncertain.

"*To make matters worse*, my husband also lost his job."

"*To make matters worse*, my dad got Covid-19 when he was in the hospital for a heart attack."

Touch base

Meaning: To check in or reconnect with someone, briefly.

Origin: It's a baseball reference, meaning to touch each base without being touched by a player with the ball.

"Can we *touch base* next week sometime? I'd love to chat more about this but I have to pick up Tim from soccer now."

"Let's *touch base* when you get back from your vacation."

The Bell and the Cat

Once upon a time there lived a group of mice. These mice were known for their intelligence and resourcefulness. In their little community, they had a wise old mouse named Oliver, who was known for sharing valuable advice.

One day, the mice gathered in the village square, expressing their concerns about a crafty cat named Cleo. Cleo was a skilled hunter, and the mice often found themselves scurrying away whenever she approached.

Oliver, with a twinkle in his eye, suggested a solution to their problem. "Let's hang a **bell** around Cleo's neck," he proposed. "This way, whenever she comes near, we will hear the bell ring, giving us time to escape before she catches us." They **crafted** a tiny bell and decided that the bravest mouse would sneak up to Cleo and tie it around her neck. The mice debated on who should undertake this risky task, but none were willing to take the challenge. The idea of facing Cleo was too frightening.

As the mice continued their discussions, they realized that coming up with a plan was one thing, but putting it into action was another. Oliver, observing their hesitation, decided to impart another piece of wisdom.

"It's not enough to have a plan; we must also be courageous enough to carry it out," Oliver advised. "Let us work together and find a way to approach Cleo without putting anyone in danger." Inspired by Oliver's words, the mice collaborated, using their collective skills to create a **distraction** while one brave mouse managed to tie the bell around Cleo's neck. Through teamwork and bravery, they successfully executed the plan.

From that day on, whenever Cleo approached, the tiny bell rang, warning the mice to scatter and find safety. The village mice learned that courage, **cooperation**, and the willingness to face challenges head-on were key to overcoming their fears.

And so, the story of the bell and the cat became a tale of teamwork and bravery, reminding everyone in the village that finding solutions required not only clever ideas but also the courage to put those ideas into action.

The Moral

The moral of the story is: "Working together and being brave can help overcome challenges and solve problems."

Vocabulary

bell: A hollow object that makes a sound.

distraction: Something that prevents one's full attention on something else.

cooperation: Working together.

crafted: Made.

Comprehension Questions

1. What was the mice's problem in the story?
2. What was Oliver's solution to the mice's problem?
3. Why were the mice hesitant to implement Oliver's plan?
4. What did Oliver remind the mice about having a plan?
5. How did the mice finally implement the plan?

Answers

1. The mice's problem was that a clever cat named Cleo liked to chase them.
2. Oliver's solution was to put a bell around Cleo's neck, so they could hear her coming and run away.
3. The mice were hesitant because tying the bell around Cleo's neck required bravery, and no mouse felt courageous enough.
4. Oliver reminded the mice that having a plan wasn't enough; they also needed courage to make it work.
5. The mice worked together, creating a distraction while one brave mouse tied the bell around Cleo's neck.

Go to War

Allan is talking about a fight with his wife.

Owen: Hey, how are things going? You look kind of upset.

Allan: My wife and I **went to war** this morning before I left for work. She **got upset** at me for not washing the dishes and **doing laundry** the night before. We're **happily married** but fight about this stuff **all the time**.

Owen: Are those your jobs?

Allan: Yes, but I **prefer to** do it on weekends while she gets it done every night. I like to **come home** from work and **have a drink** to relax. I'm **jealous of** you and your single life.

Owen: Oh, **it's not all it's cracked up to be** during a pandemic. That's for sure.

Vocabulary

went to war: A bitter fight.

got upset: Had an angry feeling.

doing laundry: Washing clothes.

happily married: A good marriage.

all the time: Always.

prefer to: Like to.

come home: Arrive at home after being out.

have a drink: Drink alcohol.

jealous of: A feeling where you want what someone else has.

it's not all it's cracked up to be: Something is not as good as it appears to be.

Practice

1. I'm so _____ his new car.

2. They seemed _____. I'm surprised to hear about their divorce.

3. When I _____, the first thing I do is take off my work clothes.

4. My kids _____ over who got to use the new video game console first.

5. I _____ eat at home instead of going out.

6. Working at Google? _____.

7. My daughter _____ when I told her that we couldn't have a party because of Covid.

8. _____ is probably my least favourite chore. There's just so much of it with the kids.

9. Let's _____ and celebrate your new job.

10. I'm trying not to think about him _____ but it's been difficult.

Answers

1. jealous of

2. happily married

3. come home

4. went to war

5. prefer to

6. it's not all it's cracked up to be

7. got upset

8. doing laundry

9. have a drink

10. all the time

Back Down

Candice is talking to Tracy about a problem at work.

Candice: I'm not going to **back down** here. It **boils down to** this—we need to fire Tony.

Tracy: Calm down. We're going to **get through** this without firing anybody.

Candice: At the very least, we need to **call in** the experts. We're not equipped to handle this.

Tracy: Why don't you take a day to **cool off**? We need to **get back to** work and keep at it. We'll **figure this out**. We've **run into** problems like this before.

Vocabulary

back down: Let up; not fight someone.

boils down to: Summarize something.

calm down: Relax; chill out.

get through: Overcome a difficult situation.

call in: Ask for help from someone.

cool off: To calm down after getting agitated or angry.

get back to: Start again; reply to a phone message or email.

figure this out: Solve a problem.

run into: See or encounter someone you have previously met.

Practice

1. I think we can _____ if we put our minds to it.

2. My son never wants to _____ and we fight to the death!

3. I hope we don't _____ Todd again. That guy is so loud.

4. Let's try to ____. I think it won't seem so bad in the morning.

5. It's time to _____ the big dogs. The guys we have just aren't getting the job done.

6. I hope that we can _____ our project soon. I hate having to deal with this other thing.

7. It _____ the fact that I just don't like working with him.

8. Please take some time to _____. We need clear heads to figure this out.

9. We're going to _____ this. I know it seems difficult but we will.

Answers

1. figure this out

2. back down

3. run into

4. calm down

5. call in

6. get back to

7. boils down to

8. cool off

9. get through

Chill Out

Keith is telling Sam that he's going to leave.

Keith: Hey, I think I'm going to **bail**.

Sam: **Chill out**! You just got here. Why are you leaving?

Keith: I'm tired of playing **third wheel** with you **couch potatoes**.

Sam: Come on, stay. We'll watch **a flick** or something.

Keith: Nah, I'm going to **roll**. I want to **catch some rays** at the beach.

Sam: You're such **a pain in the neck**! Why don't we come with you though? I'm tired of sitting around too.

Vocabulary

bail: Leave; depart.

chill out: Relax.

third wheel: Describes someone who is spending time with a couple.

couch potatoes: People who aren't that active, instead preferring to sit on the couch and watch TV or play video games.

a flick: A movie.

roll: Go somewhere.

catch some rays: Go outside in the sun.

a pain in the neck: Describes someone who is annoying or bothersome.

Practice

1. My youngest is such _____.

2. Let's _____. There are some weird people here.

3. I don't mind being the _____, depending on the couple.

4. Let's _____. We need to be there in 15 minutes.

5. I want to _____ this weekend for sure.

6. Hey, _____. We don't have to be there for another hour.

7. Do you want to catch _____ this weekend?

8. My kids are basically _____ and never want to go outside.

Answers

1. a pain in the neck

2. bail

3. third wheel

4. roll

5. catch some rays

6. chill out

7. a flick

8. couch potatoes

The Wind and the Sun

Once upon a time, in a **tranquil** meadow surrounded by towering trees and colorful flowers, there lived two friends—the Sun and the Wind. They were as different as day and night, yet their friendship was strong, and they enjoyed spending time together.

One day, the Wind and the Sun decided to have a friendly competition to see who could persuade a passing traveler to take off his heavy coat. The Wind, always eager to show off its strength, went first.

The Wind **huffed and puffed**, creating a powerful gust that rustled the leaves, swirled the dust, and howled through the meadow. The traveler, feeling the forceful wind, clutched his coat tighter and continued walking against the breeze. The Wind, frustrated by its inability to make the traveler remove his coat, **conceded** defeat. The Sun, smiling warmly, stepped forward to try its approach.

Gently, the Sun began to shine its radiant **rays** upon the meadow. The air became comfortably warm, and the traveler felt the Sun's embrace. Slowly, he started to feel the heat, and the warmth made him realize that his heavy coat was no longer necessary.

The traveler, feeling the Sun's kindness, willingly took off his coat and continued his journey with a smile. The Sun, pleased with the success of its gentle warmth, and the Wind, having learned a valuable lesson, shared a hearty laugh.

The moral of the story is that kindness and warmth can achieve what force and strength cannot. Just as the gentle Sun convinced the traveler to shed his coat, we too can achieve more through kindness and understanding than through force and power.

The Moral

The moral of the story is that being kind and gentle is often more effective than using force or being strong. Like the friendly Sun, we can achieve more by being nice to others.

Vocabulary

huffed and puffed: Breathed in a loud and heavy way.

rays: Light that comes from the sun.

tranquil: Peaceful.

conceded: Admitted defeat.

Comprehension Questions

1. What was the friendly competition between the Sun and the Wind about?

2. How did the Wind try to win the competition?

3. Why did the traveler not take off his coat when the Wind blew?

4. What approach did the Sun take in the competition?

5. What was the traveler's reaction to the Sun's approach?

Answers

1. The competition was about convincing a traveler to take off his heavy coat.

2. The Wind blew strongly, creating a powerful gust of wind.

3. The traveler held onto his coat because the Wind's force made it feel colder.

4. The Sun shone warmly and gently, creating a comfortable warmth in the meadow.

5. Feeling the Sun's kindness, the traveler willingly took off his coat and continued with a smile.

Goofing Around

Andy and Matt are talking about their kids.

Andy: How's it going these days?

Matt: Oh, I'm feeling like I might **snap** at any moment. My kids alternate between **goofing around** and **beating each other up.** I wish they'd **cut it out** and act normally.

Andy: That sounds tough. They'll **grow up** before you know it though! Enjoy it while they're young.

Matt: I know that but they **wear me down**. I hate **dealing with** their battles.

Andy: Lighten up a little! Let them **battle it out**. I know it's bad but I let my kids **get away with** murder! It helps me stay sane.

Vocabulary

snap: Get suddenly angry.

goofing around: Being silly or joking with someone.

beating each other up: Hitting or being physically violent towards each other.

cut it out: Stop doing something.

grow up: Get bigger or older.

wear me down: Make me feel tired and weary.

dealing with: Handling.

lighten up: Relax; not take things so seriously.

battle it out: Fight until there's a winner.

get away with: To do something bad but not receive punishment for it.

Practice

1. I'm not sure you should get in between them. Why not let them _____?

2. My kids _____! I need to take a walk every day to get a break.

3. Hey, stop _____. We need to get some things done.

4. You should _____. It'll be better for your mental health.

5. Kids _____ so quickly.

6. I'm going to _____ if you don't stop that.

7. The pen tapping annoys me. Please _____.

8. I know you're _____ a lot right now. Can I help by watching your kids tonight?

9. Do you think we can _____ it? I'm worried that we won't.

10. My cat and dog love _____.

Answers

1. battle it out

2. wear me down

3. goofing around

4. lighten up

5. grow up

6. snap

7. cut it out

8. dealing with

9. get away with

10. beating each other up

Before You Go

If you found this book useful, please leave a review wherever you bought it. It will help other English learners, like yourself find this resource.

You might also be interested in these books: *Advanced English Conversation Dialogues* and *The Big Book of Phrasal Verbs in Use*. Both of them are by Jackie Bolen. You can find them wherever you like to buy books. They have hundreds of helpful English phrases and expressions that can be used in a wide variety of situations. Learn to speak more fluently in American English.

17077696R00186